DOUG

Man & Missionary

The Autobiography of Doug Abrahams

OMF BOOKS

Copyright © OVERSEAS MISSIONARY FELLOWSHIP
(formerly China Inland Mission)

First printed 1983

*All rights reserved. No part of this book may be
reproduced in any way without permission from the
publishers.*

ISBN 0 85363 151 4

Published by Overseas Missionary Fellowship,
Belmont, The Vine, Sevenoaks, Kent.
TN13 3TZ, UK

Printed by Singapore National Printers (Pte) Ltd.

Contents

FOREWORD

IT WAS IN the summer of 1957, when we were missionary
candidates in the OMF Training Home in Newington
Green, that my wife and I met Doug and Olga Abrahams
for the first time. I was drawn by Doug's cheerful London
humour and warm commitment, and remember thinking
that he would be a good person to work with as a senior
missionary. Sure enough, twelve months later the OMF
sent us to work with them in Hakodate, the port city of
Hokkaido. We were still very new and raw to Japan, and
it was a tremendous help in learning the ropes to be living
next door to them. One day a visitor rattling away in
Japanese kept on drawing his hand across his throat in a
most ominous manner: was he about to slit his throat in
our living room? I kept him talking while Valerie went in
search of Doug. His arrival was a great relief, especially
when he grasped that this sob story was all a means of
begging some money off us. We had not a single Christian
alongside us at that point and, as in the work in Kutchan
and Shizunai described in this book, here there was the
same uphill struggle, the long slogging years without much
obvious fruit. Doug's cheerful optimism and Olga's cool
realism never seemed shaken by this, and in the long run a
thriving church came into existence.

Just as the birth of a baby requires months of gestation
and effort and labour, so also there has to be travail and
effort to bring a new church into existence. This book
describes the hard slogging process of starting new
congregations, in a straightforward and interesting
manner that brings everything to life, in a way that more
theoretical books about missionary principles often fail to
do.

Down the years, in spite of periods of ill health with
severe asthma, Doug has soldiered faithfully on. His

FOREWORD

account begins in the immediate post-Pacific-war years when Japan was still suffering economic depression, and life was spartan and simple compared with today's prosperous electronic Japanese society. This one missionary's lifetime of service charts the remarkable progress from small beginnings and the agonising struggles of missionaries facing all the suspicions and prejudices of the Japanese towards a foreign religion. It ends with Japanese ministers urging their missionary colleagues not to give up at this point, but to press on to build more and more new congregations by the end of the century. It also speaks of Japanese Christians being sent out as missionaries to other needy countries, to work alongside Christians from other countries. It is very encouraging to see this progress of the Gospel through the eyes of a missionary who has been in action long enough to be able to do so.

This book will also bring home to you the continuing need for missionaries today, in Japan as well as in other countries. For some strange reason, people seem to feel that people as sophisticated and courteous as the Japanese somehow need the Gospel less urgently than more obviously pagan people. But the Japanese need Christ just as much as the rest of us. They make wonderful Christians when converted, as this account makes clear. I warmly welcome this book by my old friend giving an account of God's blessing on his life and showing the need both for more missionaries and (in his final chapter) more intercessors, not only for missionaries but also for Japanese believers. If you have never had the chance to enjoy meeting Doug and Olga, this book is the next best thing.

Michael Griffiths

1

A MELANCHOLY RUSTLE

IT WAS CHRISTMAS EVE, 1946. My younger brother, Ron, and I had been on a pub crawl which had started in Wood Green and ended up in my elder brother's home in Walthamstow. Somehow the drink which should have brought me joy had gone sour on me. I suddenly despised the 'Knees up Mother Brown', the jostling crowd in the front room, the jangling piano. My temper showed in the way I flared up, and my elder brother suggested I leave for home. Ron came along with me. It was cold outside; the frost sparkled in the moon's rays on the tiles and on the railings of the front gardens. Christmas Eve — so what! There hadn't been too much 'peace on earth' these past seven years. The three mile walk home set the scene for reminiscing and wallowing in the mud of self-pity.

* * * * *

At the age of nine I was off school for two terms with pneumonia; maybe that was why I failed the equivalent of the 'eleven plus'. As a result I left school at fourteen and found a job as a messenger boy with one of England's largest advertising companies. Mum and Dad were Baptists and I had plenty of church and Sunday School . . . I wasn't ready for the new language and behaviour patterns of some of the twenty lads employed by the company. I went up to Leicester Square by 'workman's return' every morning, and played football with a tennis ball behind St Martin-in-the-Fields. We came back to the basement where we changed into our uniforms, dirty and sticky with sweat. Our job was to carry printing blocks and advertising orders to Fleet Street; I knew the London address of every local newspaper and most periodicals in the country. They pushed me on a bit, and I went to work in the newly opened commercial radio office. But when I looked for the promotion which I thought should come, it was gently explained to me that that was impossible — I did not have the necessary little bits of paper from the right school. This was the first time I had heard it put so plainly, and it hurt.

My church was a friendly one and AEB, who ran the Sunday afternoon Bible Class, was a man who gave himself to young fellows. If we missed a couple of weeks we could be sure of his measured tread coming to the house. He took us away on weekends, when we mixed his false teeth up with somebody else's and threw his hat out of the train window, but I guess he won in the end. Mrs G ran the Christian Endeavour, a group that was to train us for Christian service. I liked it because of the girls who went along, but I guess Mrs G had the last laugh, too. You can't get away from people's prayers.

At that time Mussolini had pillaged and murdered in Abyssinia, Hitler was well on the way up, and a lot of us were stirred by the doings of the International Brigade in Spain. In the meantime the Baptists solidly sang, more or less in tune:

'In heavenly love abiding
No change my heart shall fear,
And safe is such confiding
For nothing changes here.'

I'd get such a reaction as we stood in the pews on a Sunday night. Dead right we were! Nothing changes here, and it never would. But what had all this got to do with what was going on out in the world? Even so, Jesus on the Cross drew me and I was baptized when I was seventeen.

Mum used to get attacks of asthma when Ron and I, as kids, fought and yelled all over the kitchen floor. They got increasingly bad and when I was fifteen she had a thrombosis and was gone. Two years later I was best man at my father's wedding to a good Christian woman who felt she should make a home for 'us boys'. The trouble was that she didn't communicate. It was tough for her and for us. By this time I had seen something of show business; Joe Loss and his band and the cabaret in Charing Cross Road were a lot more interesting than 'heavenly love abiding'. However, as I got cleaned and dressed up on Saturday night I knew that she was going to be praying for me as soon as the front door closed behind me.

I joined the Territorial Army after Munich, and was almost glad when war broke out; we knew it had to come anyway, and I could get away from my step-mother's sad face. I think I might have made a good soldier if I hadn't been such a fool. A couple of early spells of punishment, drilling with full pack and what not, got the chips going well on my shoulder. Twice the CO gave me a stripe and twice I lost it for fighting, drunk. Once I spent a night in a civvy gaol — I had just gone back to the dance for my respirator and came out swinging it, and the copper caught it on the side of his head. The Company Sergeant Major got me out in the morning after apologies all round. Why did I have to get drunk and stupid when other men went for a quiet drink? What was it that kept driving me on? When I'd had a few beers, or a scotch or two, I felt anyone's equal; maybe that was the reason I had to drink.

I had girl friends, and got near to marriage a couple of times, but what had I got to offer? The thought that a girl might have taken me on chance of the future didn't occur to me. So I was drifting.

After Dunkirk the army hung around in England. Bored, I applied for a transfer to the Glider Pilot Regiment. We reported for training and they started on us. It was tough. Bull, bull and more bull, and assault courses, and marching and doubling, and ridiculous inspections. They had plenty of volunteers, and they were out to bust those that couldn't take it. Anybody could ask for a transfer back to his former unit without prejudice. I kept going for a week or two, but two little things broke me. I hadn't got a change of clothing because my laundry hadn't come through, and I got a real snorter of a cold. I reported to the duty officer and he really blistered me, but I couldn't keep going on the training, so I was back to unit.

Some funny things happened, funny peculiar, I mean. Just before D-Day we had a church parade. We didn't actually parade; they had stopped those things. But we all turned up to the church services in a big hall. The preacher was a tall chap and fairly young. The few padres I had seen had had last war medals and a desire to tell us to do a good job, men! Presumably by that they meant kill a few Huns. But this man was different; he had no medals and wore a long black gown with a couple of white bits sticking out at the neck. He was concerned about something; you could tell that by the way he spoke. He was warning us that we might well be meeting with God in a few days or even hours, and were we ready? I thought about the way some of those old Baptist preachers had let go on Sunday nights in West Green, Tottenham. Still, hell or heaven was a bit under the belt at this stage, but if what he said was right then he wasn't dodging the issue of letting us know. Most of us were quiet for a bit, but once more in the barracks, waiting for D-Day, we were soon back at the cards.

We got to a place called Vernon on the Seine, where our detachment had to look after a Bailey bridge. Our section officer let a couple of us off into the town each night. The French were treating us, like heroes and we'd come up the road full of Calvados. I went into town with a fellow from Shef- field and we were nicely oiled, singing a little, on our way back to the bridge. Suddenly he stopped and turned to me; 'You ain't like me,' he said. 'I don't believe in no God; when you're finished, you're finished, that's what I think. But you believe in God.' That shook me a bit because I couldn't see where he got the information from. I certainly wasn't acting as if I believed in Him.

We pushed into Belgium and were billeted in Ghent. It was Christmas Eve, and I was a lance jack. The Company Sergeant Major said to me, 'Bring another corporal over to the sergeants' mess tonight and we'll have a couple of bottles of cognac for the lads.' So we did. Inside the sergeants' mess we had quite a few drinks and I started out from there with a bottle of cognac in each pocket of my greatcoat. I have never remembered what happened after that. I can remember lying down in a field. There was a severe frost and the ground was hard and white with rime, but I was strangely warm, and it seemed an ideal spot to go to sleep. Then somebody was slapping my face and kicking me to my feet and getting me onto the road, getting me walking. Maybe it was an angel; maybe it was a Belgian. Angel means 'God's messenger', anyway, doesn't it? If left, I would have been dead.

The bottles of cognac were smashed and the lads were browned off. I felt really bad. I couldn't even handle a little job like getting the lads their Christmas drink without fouling it up.

I was demobbed in the spring of 1946. Six and a half years wasted; nothing achieved. The advertising company, true to their promise, took me back, but at that stage my job was non-existent and the money they paid me hardly met my tube fares and lunches.

What future was there? I changed my job and worked as a wages clerk for a small building firm. I also began reading the Bible, I don't know why. I made sure my stepmother didn't know about it — I guess I didn't want her to think she was winning. I got a Moffat's translation out of the local library and became absorbed in it. Those crazy Hebrews, no matter what Moses or God did for them, neither Moses nor God could please them. Why didn't God just blast them off the face of the earth? Then a voice inside me said, 'You are just like one of those Hebrews'. I went right through all the Old Testament on into the New. I had heard the stories of Jesus before in my Sunday School days, but it sure rang a bell this time. The things Christ said were absolutely right. The things He did were absolutely right. And then they killed Him. That was right, too. A Man as good as that couldn't go on living in our kind of world. Then there was the resurrection.

I had a friend who had fallen off his bicycle when he was eighteen trying to avoid a little girl who had run out in front of him. He had become slowly, incurably paralysed. When I came out of the army he was prostrate and sometimes I took him into the park in a bed on wheels. He could talk a bit, and he'd talk about what a wonderful Saviour he had in Jesus. Once I blew my top. 'Look,' I said, 'you say you are a sinner and Jesus has saved you. How do you get that way? You can't even walk across the room. How can you say you are a sinner? Seems to me God is a bit unjust to put this on you.' He would just give a gentle smile and leave me shattered. But this I could see: if there was no life after death then this life was one hideous joke brought about by some maniac mind. If there was life after death, in some form or other, and this cripple was better fitted for eternity than I, then he was plus, wasn't he?

There was a new minister down at West Green. He was on the small side, didn't wear a dog collar, and used ordinary language without any haw-haw. He had come from Ebbw Vale and understood the sufferings of the unemployed. We started a soccer team and he came and played in it. In the dressing rooms on Lea Marshes the news got around that a parson was playing and he had quite a kick. It was funny why I went back to church. I wasn't sure about anything and often I'd get a skinful on Saturday and be in the church pew the next morning. The old folk must have smelt the liquor but there was never a turning of the shoulder, only smiles of welcome. One night the minister said very earnestly from the pulpit, 'Eternal life is God's gift; it's not just something after death; it's new life now; you can have it now.' I didn't see it that way. I figured I needed to clean things up a bit before I started a proper Christian life.

The two obvious things to start on were beer and fags. So I'd stop smoking on Monday and last out until Thursday and then I'd give in. I stopped drinking for a bit, but then I'd start again. By now I'd discovered from the Bible that every little sin would have to be accounted for, so I was really heading for trouble! Man, how could I get right? Sometimes, I'd lie awake at nights thinking about things. What good was I? What was the future? Was there really a God and, if so, what then?

* * * * *

So we walked back from Walthamstow to Tottenham that Christmas Eve, mulling over the past. I read somewhere, 'The leaves of memory have a melancholy rustle', and I guess that was it. Nobody understood us, there was no future for us, we didn't fit in. That's how we felt. And we decided to pray. I'm not sure how we got to that decision but suddenly it had been made. We quickened our steps up the road. Ron dug into his pocket for the key and we stepped into the house and switched on the light. We tried to be quiet because we didn't want the old folks coming down. We dropped on our knees. We had never done this before and I felt a bit daft. There wasn't anybody there to hear our prayers but I got suddenly determined. 'God,' I said, 'If there is a God, and Jesus Christ is His Son, then here I am for what I am worth. Over to you.' I don't know what my brother prayed or whether I had prayed out loud or not. I meant this prayer as I had never meant anything in my life before. Then we stood up and went to bed.

2

A NEW START

THE OLD BEDROOM looked the same that Christmas morning. The disused gas bracket on the wall with a flowered text hanging on it — 'Thou art my God, early will I seek thee' This had been the old lady's attempt to get me religious, I reckon, but I'd never pulled the thing down. When we were kids bugs had got into the old wooden bed and would bite us until we got inured to it. The bugs used to run up the wall and Ron and I would kill them, leaving smears of red blood on the wallpaper. Finally Dad had lugged the bed downstairs into the garden and burned the thing, and we had watched the bugs come out of the wood as it got too warm for them, and run this way and that trying to find a way out. I guess that there hadn't been any way out for them. It had been bugging me for years that there wasn't any way out for me. But now there was.

I've heard hundreds of people speak of what Jesus means to them, and of how He found them. It's like trying to play some wonderful piece of music on a mouth organ — you can't get all the sounds in. That morning I knew I was saved, changed, everything was different. Right down inside me was a great big chunk of joy that I couldn't keep to myself. I belonged to God. He had taken me in from the cold outside. Jesus had died for me! Fancy a Man like Jesus, Who was God's Son, dying for a bloke like me! This really gripped me.

An old mate of mine came to the door and knocked, and when he saw my face he looked kind of quizzical. 'I'm saved,' I said, not knowing what else to say, 'You look it,' he said.

There were all kinds of variations on the theme. Maybe I had been a Christian before but had turned my back on God's love and decided that I'd go where I wanted to go, thank you very much. Maybe I was like the man in the story that Jesus tells who went into a far country, taking all that his Dad had given him and wasting the lot. Then, when he was really down and out, he came home. His Dad had been sitting in the front room watching out of the window, and when he saw this rough looking drop-out coming back he recognized his boy and went dashing out of the front door to drag him in and make him feel he was back where he ought to be. Anyway I knew where I was now. God lived. God had heard my prayer and He had welcomed me, just as I was.

There didn't seem to be any need for the beer any more. I had Jesus. He walked with me. I knew He was right there although I couldn't see Him. I had to tell my mates about this and of course they would know I wasn't kidding them, and they'd come home too, and we would all have Christ in our hearts and soon the whole world would be believing in Jesus. But it wasn't that easy. I saw three of the lads I'd known for years coming up the road and I stopped them. Soon I could see I wasn't getting across. They weren't turned on. They looked uneasy and seemed anxious to get away. 'Well,' said one in a distant sort of way, 'it's time you turned over a new leaf and buckled down to things instead of griping and boozing, but we don't get the religious stuff.' And they walked away.

I had been a church member ever since I was seventeen, which meant I got in on church meetings where they discussed the programme. Some of us had been pushing for some time for something to liven up the programme. How about using the up-stairs hall for some dancing? That would bring the young people into the church, and we would make a profit on the dances, and the whole thing would mushroom. Only one or two old religious fogeys were standing in the way, and we had reckoned that at the next meeting we'd have a lot to say about getting a lively programme. But between one meeting and the next Jesus had come into my heart, and suddenly I saw all sorts of things I hadn't seen before. I found myself with the religious fogeys and enjoying it! We didn't have any dances, but instead we got the prayer meeting warmed up. That was another thing — I found out that I liked praying with people. It didn't matter whether they were young or old, men or women, beautiful or ugly, rich or poor, just as long as they loved God and wanted to pray with me. And God answered our prayers.

I wanted to tell others about Jesus and the cross and all but didn't know where to start. So I decided to wear a Christian badge. I figured that when some of those hefty building operatives and works managers came into the wages office they'd see the thing, challenge me, and we'd get right in. But this didn't happen. What did happen was that the little blonde who worked there took one look and said in a soft voice, 'Oh, 'ave you gone all religious?' Funnily enough, I found that hard to take and wanted to deny Him, but I managed some sort of a positive answer.

The Bible was a new book to me now, and I just wanted to spend hours studying it and pass on what I learnt! So I started preaching right away but hadn't a clue how to start and when to finish, nor could I get my ideas straight. I'd just get up on my feet and shout my head off. One of the older men in the church put me in my place. 'Your zeal' he said, 'is greater than your knowledge.' I wanted to get more Bible knowledge, but I couldn't see the way and it didn't occur to me to talk it over with the minister.

A young couple who had been keen Christians for years lived near me, and I used to go to their home night after night, reading the Bible, praying, and telling them what God was doing for me. Then one day I read in the Bible, 'Go not too often to a friend's house' and that hit me like a ton of bricks. Here was this young couple, separated for years through the war, looking for a bit of peace and quiet and opportunity to get together and make up on lost time, and here was me playing gooseberry breaking up their joy. I didn't go for a month or more and they wondered why I stopped coming, but we finally sorted that one out.

Round about that time we formed a group, working out from the Christian Endeavour, for evangelism. We would stand around Turnpike Lane Tube Station witnessing and talking to people, and sometimes we'd speak to the crowds queueing up for the cinema. One night a bus inspector was listening quite patiently to my friend's wife and at the end he said, 'You know what — I think that what you are doing is good, but you'll never get yourself a husband that way.' With a winning smile Mrs O said, 'Would you like to talk to my husband? He's over there.' 'OK, you win,' said the bus inspector.

The Bible worked on me — having found Jesus I didn't want to lose the way again. I took the Bible literally. One day, kneeling on the floor with my Bible on the bed, I was reading in Leviticus in the Old Testament. All the ancient laws for getting right with God are there. I read, 'If any one sins and commits a breach of faith against the Lord by deceiving his neighbour in a matter of deposit or security, or through robbery . . . when one has sinned and become guilty, he shall restore what he took by robbery.' All this hadn't much to do with me, I thought. One thing I hadn't done was steal things. I'd kept my hands off other people's property. Still, the teaching was good and right, and I'd remember it. I got up to go to the cupboard and there they were — several sets of underwear that I had taken from a QM store when I left the army! They were to set me up with winter wear for ten years or more. But they weren't mine. I had stolen them. Now, wait a minute, you couldn't really say that. You couldn't steal things from the army. It wasn't the same as stealing from people. Besides, I had given the army seven years. I didn't owe them anything. No, Leviticus chapter 6 verses one to six didn't apply to army underwear.

Or did it? When I got back from the builder's office that night I opened the Bible, but it didn't mean anything to me. All I could think about was that underwear. I tried praying but I couldn't. Army underwear or Jesus, one or the other but I couldn't have both. Sounds crazy, but there you are. Most people would have got rid of that underwear quick as lightning, but I hung on to it for three or four days. It was quite a battle. I tried to rationalize the whole thing, and in any case where could I send it to a year after demob? Finally, I gave in. I packed the whole lot in some old brown paper, tied it up with string and sent it to the War Office, Whitehall, with a note inside saying why I was doing it. What the bloke at the other end thought when he opened that parcel, I'll never know, but the Bible came alive again.

I was getting more and more to see the importance of faith, of believing in Jesus Christ, God's Son. If He said He was the way and the truth and the life, if He was the One Who forgave us our sins, if He was the One Who died on the cross for us, if He was the way to God, then there was nothing more important than this. This was more important than anything else — riches, education, fame, health, or anything. God had come as a baby in Jesus, lived in Galilee, had been killed on a cross ànd came back from the dead. Those who believed this received the Spirit of

Jesus, and the Bible told us it was right; so did the church. When I say the 'church', I don't mean the Lambeth Conference or the World Council of Churches; I mean people. I realized this just after I had had a rough time trying to convince some of my relatives that religion was real, and also some of my mates had made it clear that they didn't want to know. A rather clever man had almost convinced me that I might be heading for religious mania, and that the whole thing was in the mind anyway. That week I met five men — a doctor, a baker's roundsman, a high school teacher, an office clerk and a carpenter. I had never met these men before, and culturally we didn't have too much in common with each other, but they all confirmed to me what had happened in me. We had the same Spirit, the Spirit of Jesus Christ. Since that day I have met hundreds if not thousands of people of all nationalities — Japanese, Chinese, Filipinos, Indians, Germans, Americans, Africans, you name them — and they have the same Spirit of Jesus received through faith in Him. That's what I mean by the witness of the church to Christ, the Risen Christ.

We had a missionary Sunday at the church. The missionary didn't send me too much. He worked in India; my brother had been to India and they had an argument about Hinduism. The missionary seemed to think that sincerity was the main thing, and my brother didn't. The missionary reckoned that it was OK for the Hindu to pray to his gods and us to pray to ours. My brother didn't, and he said so in good old cockney which left the missionary gasping for breath. Maybe my brother should have been more gracious.

We had a prayer meeting afterwards, just an old deacon who had been in the first world war, five ladies all over fifty, and me. The old deacon said, 'I think that someone in this meeting is called to the mission field.' When he said that, I opened one eye and looked around the assembled company. I couldn't see any of those ladies going to the mission field because they had husbands and families and maybe grandchildren to look after. On the other hand I wasn't doing anything special. I wasn't tied by holy matrimony yet. I guessed he must mean me, and it was OK with me, at least it was at that point, because I hadn't any idea what I was going to get involved in.

I saw the gentleman a few days later walking down the street and crossed the road to talk to him. 'You know what you said at that meeting about God calling somebody to the mission field? Well, what do I do?' He seemed very pleased indeed although I couldn't see what the excitement was about. 'I can introduce you to the secretary of a missionary society,' he said, and that is what he did. The secretary was a clergyman with a very wide dog collar, and he was very helpful. He began to talk to me about guidance, and I hadn't too much of it. I didn't know what country God was calling me to or what I would do when I got there. He must have thought me pretty stupid, which I was. 'You will need to go to Bible School. Do you think you can learn a foreign language? Have you read much on missions?' I had never studied a foreign language except a form of French which consisted of 'voulez vous promenader avec moi' and they usually didn't. I had also learnt to say 'verboten' in German.

At that moment the mission field seemed a long way away. It seemed to be a little more complicated than just getting on a boat and going. Yet the idea stuck. People ought to know about Jesus. There were fewer people telling people about Him overseas, and most people in England could hear if they wanted to.

About this time I got hold of a book which made a lasting impression on me, and I think God wanted me to read it. It was the life story of a man called C T Studd. He had been an All England cricketer, was one of the landed gentry and had a fortune, but gave it away and took Christ to China, India and Africa. He felt that if he was doing the work that God wanted him to do, then God would look after His end of it and supply the things needed in this life like food and clothing and a place to live. God says 'Seek first the kingdom of God and all these things shall be added unto you'. In the days when C T Studd travelled around things were rough, but God kept all His promises to him. This book thrilled me. I can't explain my feelings. It was as though this was what I had been looking for. Here was somebody who took the promises in the Bible and just got going on them. This process was called living by faith.

I spoke to my stepmother about it. In spite of our different natures, since I had changed we could now communicate. But she got scared at the way I was talking. 'Look,' she said, 'you can't just pack up work. You have to work for your living.' I could see that at that point we weren't communicating. 'Yes, but if God is calling us to live trusting Him for everything then that's OK, isn't it?' More and more it was apparent that, as C T Studd said, 'If Jesus Christ was God's Son, and died for me, then nothing that I do can be great enough.' But how did I start? I hadn't played for England and I didn't have a fortune to give away. I was just a little cog. Through the spring of 1947 I was keeping on with my job at the builders' office, making casual friendships with Christian girls, playing football on Saturdays, witnessing in open air meetings, but down inside was this conflict of faith.

I knew I wanted to do two things — to study the Bible and to preach its message. Now, this mission field angle and C T Studd's betting all on God had come to add fuel to the fire. I opened my Bible to a story about Gideon. The Israelites as usual were in trouble because they had forgotten God and gone after other gods. Then, when they were really down, they had shouted to God to help them out of trouble. To do this God was preparing a man called Gideon. A messenger from God approached Gideon while he was hiding out. 'The Lord is with you, you mighty man of valour,' said the angel. Maybe Gideon was looking round to see who this mighty man of valour was, because he wasn't feeling too brave. Anyway, he made a few excuses. 'How can I deliver Israel? Look, my clan is the weakest in Manasseh, and I am the least in my own family.' Then the messenger went on to say that the operative word is 'God'. If

God is for us . . . This part of the Bible really registered with me at that time. I was like Gideon all right, just a nobody. Who was I to go around telling people to get delivered from Satan and turn to God? Yet God could use anybody if He wanted to. But did He want to use me? Did I have any guidance, as the missionary society secretary had asked me weeks before? Wait a minute. Maybe this very part of the Bible was the guidance God was trying to give me!

I made my application to All Nations Bible College, the place that had been suggested to me as majoring on missionary training. Although I didn't know where the road was going to lead, this was the way, I was sure. I hadn't got too much money, and I would have to find fees for Bible School for three years, it seemed. Then I'd need books, clothes and so on. I knew I wasn't going to go round asking for money but would ask God in prayer. If He was calling me then He would supply. I found this difficult to talk to people about. It was something between me and my heavenly Father.

I had some money in the bank. Some of it was money which I had sent home during the war, and part of my war gratuity was left. I estimated that this would last a year with care. It was basic in living by faith, that at the beginning you handed everything over to God and that was that.

It was on a bright September morning that I packed my few belongings in a pack, put the pack on my back, got on my old Hercules bicycle and cycled out to the North Circular Road, having decided that I would cycle round that way to Ealing, on to

Slough and then Taplow, the home of All Nations Bible College.

3

DISCOVERIES IN BIBLE COLLEGE

THE SUNDAY NIGHT before I left for Bible College the church gave me a good send off, saying they would be behind me in prayer. They agreed that God was calling me into His service. I didn't quite get the gist of all this because I reckoned that we were all in God's service. The minister had been a bit down because I hadn't talked to him about going to the mission field, and why wasn't I going to a Baptist college? It just hadn't occurred to me to ask him about things. He was a busy man and I didn't want to bother him. Only a long time afterwards did I realize how upset he may have been, because many times he had helped me from tripping up in my Christian life. As for going to a Baptist college, well, nobody had asked me. However, we did fix up an interview with a man in charge of missions, but we didn't communicate. He didn't know it, but his accent was against him for a start, and then he went on about two years to get my matric, and then three years or more in Bible college. I could see myself getting to preach the Gospel when I was about due for a pension. On top of that, he didn't ask me what to me was very important — whether I was saved or not. Let's put it down to God knowing what He was doing, and leave it at that.

At the end of the evening service the church gave me a cheque for £50. This shook me and I was just full of joy and glory because the church was with me. At the same time I didn't want the money like this, and I talked to my brother Ron about it. I didn't see that this was living by faith, and said so. 'Ho ho,' said he, 'and what do you think should happen — a brick come through the window with fifty quid attached with a message on it from God?' I got the point.

All Nations Bible College consisted of about thirty men studying, three lecturers who lived in the building with us, and other people who came along to tell us about things from time to time. The building itself was an old country house with lots of rooms. From the window upstairs you could look down the slopes to the Thames. There were outhouses and barns, and wide oblong lawns.

There were people from all denominations there. Methodists, Anglicans, Brethren, Baptists, Pentecostalists and others. I had a real hang up on the Anglicans. I had never met an Anglican Christian before, and to me they were part of the Establishment. Where I came from there were three Anglican churches and they all had incense-swinging capers which I had always regarded as highly suspicious. Then there was a story in our family about my grandfather. He was a herdsman and had been born and bred in a small Cambridgeshire village. One day a man had come to the village with a Bible under his arm and a message that all must be born again. My grandfather and others had believed him and they met regularly in an old tin shack. The vicar had been upset about this and had had a word with the squire. All the people in the village got a good piece of meat from the squire to see them through the hard winter months. But not those four or five strange dissidents! Then there was the business of baptizing infants. How could the eternal destiny of a tiny baby be decided by sprinkling a few drops of water on him! But here they were in All Nations, Anglicans they were and Christians they were! I'd got to adjust in a hurry. These Anglicans knew Jesus as their Saviour and Lord, no doubt about it.

All these men had a sense of 'call', that is, they felt that God had a work for them to do, probably somewhere abroad. Almost all of them were ex-servicemen, Army, Navy or RAF. Through the war years many of them had stood for Christ and had proved their faith. Some had been prisoners of war. All were trusting God for their future.

The Bible School had lectures every morning Monday to Friday; afternoons were generally given over to outdoor subjects like gardening or carpentry, or something else regarded as useful for a missionary to know. One afternoon during the week we had a service and there were prayer meetings for foreign missions. Saturday was a free day, but Sunday was for worship. Evenings we studied what we had learned during the lectures. That was the general run of things.

The atmosphere of this College hit me like an avalanche. In some ways it was like the army, and yet so different. No obscene language, no dirty jokes but plenty of clean ones, no perpetual sex talk, no lies, and yet a manliness beyond doubt. These men loved one another as Jonathan loved David, each giving the other pre-eminence, none looking for advantage, serving one another. I had never been anywhere like it before. I longed to be accepted by these men, not realizing that I already was.

My first three days in the place were days of turmoil. I felt unclean amongst these men. I could see things like pride in me, and not in them. And then there were the lectures. I had never sat in a lecture room in my life before. I didn't know what to do, or where to start! I had a pen and some paper in front of me on the desk, and when I noticed the guy next to me starting to write something down I reckoned I'd better do the same. I began to write feverishly, seeking to get every word down, but I had to give up. Then for about twenty minutes I just sat and tried to enjoy what the lecturer was saying — I couldn't understand a lot of it. It took me quite a time to learn to take notes! Then the books! I picked up a volume of Hodges Systematic Theology. How I longed to get this inside me! I opened the book at page one and read. At the end of the page I knew there were things I just hadn't understood. What was a 'phenomenon' anyway? I shoved the book back onto the shelf. Half of me wanted to put All Nations as far from me as the east is from the west, and the other half was revelling in the friendship, comradeship, call it what you will, of these students, together with the opportunity to study the Bible.

We had our first football match, against a team

from another Bible School. To my astonishment, before the game both sides lined up and we had a word of prayer. These fellows even prayed before a football game. This was really the Kingdom of God! I have since learned that there is something about theological students when they get on a football pitch. If they didn't start with prayer they'd all get killed! I haven't known from that day to this what really happened to me. Some of the players say that I was going after the ball and upended and dived into the ground. Whatever it was I went out like a light and they carried me off the field. I didn't come round for quite a bit and couldn't remember who or what I was for some hours. This accident slowed me down a bit and maybe kept me from jumping on my bike and heading for home.

Man is a social animal and there is nothing like swopping stories. I had my share of war experiences, just a little exaggerated, always putting me in the limelight, and I could tell the stories well. The other fellows enjoyed the relaxation and I enjoyed being the centre of attention. Then one of our Tuesday afternoon speakers talked about Aachan. Israel attacked Ai, and was defeated. When the chips were down it was shown that they were defeated not because of the outward opposition but because of the inward canker. One of the Israelites had helped himself to the loot against God's express orders, and this was why they had lost the battle. The speaker pointed out that a group of Christians are the body of Christ. If one part of that body is in the wrong with God then the whole body suffers. As the man was speaking I felt myself getting smaller and smaller inside because I could see I was Aachan. Not that I had taken any of the loot, but I had been building up my ego. I felt that I needed to do something about it but didn't know what. I prayed about it. I just felt that if the trekking teams went out preaching that weekend without me putting things right then there would be no help from God, and I believed it was the Holy Spirit Who was teaching me this. Any sin of the individual will affect the whole church of God. There was an early morning prayer meeting on Saturday, and I went to it and asked if I could say something. The students were all waiting, and I told them that the yarns I had told them weren't strictly truthful and I was just trying to call attention to my self, that I felt I ought to confess this to them and would they forgive me. I also went to the Principal and told him about it. They all took it in their stride but it cost me a lot and humbled me quite a bit.

I discovered three things in Bible School. The first in order was 'first causes'. The Principal, the Rev. Brash Bonsall, will forgive me if I say that to us he was very erratic and yet he taught me, and I think the rest, the importance of first causes. Simply speaking, it means that God is in absolute and direct control of the individual's situation. Whatever the problem or trouble, God has a purpose in it. If we have an accident then God has an overruling purpose. If the person next to us is an awkward person then it is because we need to have him there. Linked with this 'doctrine' is the importance of prayer, for we can only discover God's purpose in this thing by prayer. The bursting of the boiler then becomes a great adventure! Life at ANBC in those days was a great adventure.

The second thing I discovered was the principle of faith. I learned that God guides and directs individuals according to their own personality. There were two men I admired tremendously. Both had been army men, one had been a prisoner of war. One's attitude to finance was, 'I will not spend a penny above what I need' and he certainly would not spend what he didn't have. We heard that on one occasion he had not written to his wife, who was studying in another Bible School, for six weeks because they hadn't the money. A word to any of us would have brought a stamp, but he and she regarded this as a discipline from God. I felt that this was really something and tried to follow it. I scrupulously watched every ha'penny. But under this discipline I didn't have the peace he had. The other man's attitude was 'I have a heavenly father, and He is not a pauper'. He certainly didn't waste things or money but he had an easy attitude to things. I tried to follow him but discovered I hadn't the discernment he had. By trying to strike a balance, in prayer and Bible study, I found the way that I thought God would have me to go. I have never gone into debt; I have never appealed for funds, but for 24 years God has supplied my needs.

The third thing I discovered was the China Inland Mission! It began when, in my second term, I read 'The Growth of a Soul' by Mrs Howard Taylor. Soon after starting at All Nations I had heard of the scores of foreign missions that were reaching out to Africa, South America, Asia and the Isles of the Sea. Some of the students were strong advocates of the missions that they felt God was calling them to, and literature would be left in obvious places for the uncommitted. I was one of the uncommitted. At that stage I was expecting to go overseas, but where and with what society I had no idea. I prayed in a general way. C T Studd had set my sails, now Hudson Taylor got me in orbit! 'The Growth of a Soul' and its sequel 'The Growth of a Work of God' really spoke to me. C T Studd was the great dashing cavalry leader, a Rupert of Missions or General Patton. Hudson Taylor was maybe the Lord Alexander or General Eisenhower. The principles of the mission which came out of the suffering which Hudson Taylor underwent spoke to my soul. These principles, for a faith mission, were right. No appeal for funds, no going into debt, the belief that God's work done in God's way would not lack God's supply. These were basic. The sufferings and the courage of the early pioneers in China thrilled me. I could see the dust on those Honan plains, the pigtailed Chinese, the wayside inns, the preaching in the market places, the jostling multitudes, the awful need. Hudson Taylor had even been to Tottenham and found a haven there amongst the people called Brethren! Slowly, yet with a sense of humility, the conviction came that I should make some approach to this China Inland Mission.

In those days foreign missionary societies had their annual meetings in May and some students went up to three or four meetings. They had an interest in all missions! Finally, even Brash put his foot down. No going up to town in May to attend missionary meetings unless the student had made some approach to that society. One morning I walked into another man's room and there on his bed was a notice, 'China Inland Mission Annual Meeting'. The meeting was that day. It would be nice to go, it would be helpful to go, maybe it was important for me to go, but Brash wouldn't wear that one. I hadn't said to anyone that I was interested in China and the CIM. But by mid-morning the conviction I should go to the meeting had strengthened, so between lectures I tapped on the door of the Principal's office. 'Come in,' said the high-pitched voice within. I walked in and began to mumble something about the meeting in town. Knowing Brash I should have been prepared but I wasn't. Before I had got halfway through my prepared speech the Principal had slid off his seat, was in a kneeling position and was praying out loud. 'This, Lord, is what you have been leading your servant to . . .' I cannot remember all the prayer now, but off I went to the meeting.

The Westminster Central Hall was pretty full but I was able to get a seat. After some singing the speakers began. The first was the Finance Secretary, Mr F Keeble. He had held the secrets of God's supply for nearly a thousand missionaries, and what he had to say held my attention. A doctor came on next stressing the need for medical workers, and yet a third left me a bit flat. All China needed, it seemed, was one or two people who had special training. Then the fourth, a young woman, began to speak. She had been a draper's assistant before going to China and the Home Director had put her mind at rest by saying that she would have more important things to sell now. She told of the masses without the simplest knowledge of Christ, the women, the children, the men, the farmers, business people, and the students of China, and she told how God had used her among them. And God spoke to me through her.

When I got back to the Bible College, I learned that the CIM was a bit of an élite among missions. It was thought that without a university degree you hadn't a hope of being accepted. I wasn't too concerned — I would apply and see what happened. So I wrote to Mr Bentley-Taylor, the Candidate Secretary. I think I said something to the effect that I had been a Christian for many years, had backslidden a bit during the war years but God had restored me, and I was now in ANBC. I felt that the Lord was calling me to China with the CIM. At the same time I couldn't quite see what future there was in it as the people of China seemed to be pretty well evangelized. (This was indeed the impression I had got from three of the four speakers.) Then I waited for the reply. The CIM handled its mail promptly and efficiently. 'Dear Mr Abrahams . . . the idea that China is adequately evangelized should be stoutly resisted.' Anybody who knew David Bentley-Taylor as I came to know him would realize that he would stoutly resist anything of that nature! So I was started on the way to China.

The CIM suggested that I come up for an initial

interview, and things began to move. Then the College had one of its half-night prayer meetings. Whenever there was some special financial need, or some evangelistic effort, or the spiritual life of the college was getting a bit formal, we had a half-night of prayer to warm things up a bit. I always enjoyed them. I like praying in a loud voice, and banging on the chair (we used to kneel on the floor with our heads and hands on the chairs) and saying 'Amen' any place in the prayers without waiting for the end. On this particular night I began what could be described as a conversation with my conscience, although it seemed more like a conversation with the Lord. It went like this:

Conscience: That was a good letter you wrote to the CIM, wasn't it?

Me: Yes, it wasn't bad, was it?

Conscience: You didn't quite tell the truth, did you?

Me: What do you mean by that?

Conscience: You didn't tell them about being a drunkard and blasphemer for a long time, did you?

Me: No, I didn't, but did I need to? I told them I had backslidden, didn't I?

Conscience: But suppose the CIM accepts you and then you get out there and things get tough and you go on the beer again?

Me: But God can keep me, can't He?

Conscience: You'd better let 'em know what you were.
(This was a statement, not a question.)

(All the time this was going on we were having a great old prayer meeting, with people praying for power and blessing and help, and praising the Lord for His goodness and mercy and so on.)

Me: But if I write and tell them all that, then they'll turn me down flat, won't they?

Conscience: And what does that matter? The thing for you to do is to walk in the light.

I knew what 'conscience' was getting at. The Bible says, 'If we walk in the light as He is in the light we have fellowship with one another and the blood of His Son cleanses us from all sin.' You can't have real fellowship without being honest; if you keep things hidden you'll be heading for trouble.

So off went the letter explaining what a weakling I had been and pointing out the risk of having anything to do with a bloke like me. I received a good reply from D Bentley-Taylor. Whether intentionally or not the letter began warmly with, 'Dear Brother . . .'

All Nations Bible College students were interested in the value of a soul. That's the way they put it. They figured that if Jesus Christ, the Son of God, was prepared to suffer on Calvary to save men and women from hell, then men and women must be pretty valuable. What they were interested in was what Christ Himself was interested in. 'What shall it profit a man if he gain the whole world and lose his own soul: what shall a man give in exchange for his soul.' Today I hear a lot about the whole man — the church ought to be interested in the whole man —

there is something in that. But when the whole man has been fed, clothed, educated, housed and medicated, it is still his soul, that inner man, that needs to be brought back to God. This was the emphasis in ANBC. And this was what I wanted to do, to bring men back to God. Some free afternoons I would walk out around those Buckinghamshire hedges and find some quiet spot and open my Bible. I wanted power, power to live a clean life, power to witness to the world about a Saviour, power to preach the Gospel. I longed to see the Spirit of God convicting men of their need and bringing them to Christ. Sometimes I'd forget where I was and cry audibly in prayer to the Lord. I scared at least one old farmer in this way, and I don't think my apology reassured him too much!

All Nations was interested in revival too. We felt that the church in England was dead and getting deader. Men were crying 'peace, peace, when there was no peace' and it was up to All Nations to do something about it. We prayed and worked for revival. We studied movements of the Spirit of the past. Wesley, Finney, the 1859 revival which began in a prayer meeting in New York and swept across Northern Ireland and on into England, the revival in Wales in 1904. We had some experiential knowledge of the blessing of God on the church in Ruanda in the 1940s, when God had moved in quickening blessing and in the fire of the Holy Spirit into the Anglican work in that part of Africa. The great men of prayer of the past — Murray McCheyne, Jonathan Goforth, Praying Hyde and others — we studied their secrets. Great preachers — Moody, Spurgeon, Savonarola — we longed to emulate. We believed simply yet profoundly that God was able to work in sovereign power in answer to prayer. Education was a help but wasn't necessary in God's economy. Spurgeon was self-taught, Moody's grammar was bad, Billy Bray could hardly read or write but he had turned Cornwall upside down. We sought after the secrets of God.

Correspondence with the CIM Candidate Secretary continued, and soon it was suggested that I should spend a weekend at Highbury New Park, near the headquarters of the Mission in Newington Green. The Mission wanted to give me the once-over! I made my way up there on the old bicycle and knocked on the door of the big old house. The hall was wide and the floor covered with well-polished linoleum. I was shown to a room upstairs. It was already dark outside and the light was on in the room. There was a small bed ready made up, a chair, and a small rather ancient chest of drawers. On the wall was a text with a China motif as a background. There was also some Chinese writing on the wall. I felt (a) I was on holy ground and (b) I was already getting to China. Then the light went out! I couldn't see a thing. I had put my bag on the bed but couldn't get my bearings. I found the door and stepped outside, wondering what I was getting into.

There on the third step of the wide centre stairs was an apparition. In its hand was a long candle in a candlestick. It wore a long sweeping Chinese gown,

the flickering candle rays accentuating high cheek
bones, yellowish features, piercing dark black eyes
and long black hair which swept back, nearly down
to the waist. I expected to hear the hound of the
Baskervilles any minute. The apparition spoke in a
pleasant voice. 'We shall meet in happier circum-
stances in the morning, Mr Abrahams.' A candle
was given to me and the apparition glided up the
stairs. I beat a hasty retreat into my room. The next
morning, Mrs Bentley-Taylor, who had so
graciously hastened to bring me some kind of light,
looked quite different. This is all I remember about
that visit except the large picture in the hall of
Hudson Taylor, beard, long hair and all.

Gradually my philosophy of faith and works had
evolved: if I feel that God is calling me to some
service without outward support then He will supply
by some other means. Otherwise I should expect to
work in ordinary ways. My summer vacations were
a bit of a mixture. Plenty of organizations were
ready to use a Bible School student living by faith.
As he lived by faith, presumably his board was
sufficient for him. Somehow, my old bolshie
background caused me to react against this. 'A
labourer is worthy of his hire' is not a bolshie precept
but a Christian one. I spent two summers with the
Rev. Ely and his family who ran a camp near Poole,
Dorset. He hired the land, the tents and a big
marquee and he paid us well; does that sound
mercenary! Youth organizations such as Boys'
Brigade, Girls' Life Brigade, Campaigners and so on
came and used the facilities. Mr Ely and his team

provided the meals which were cooked in field kitchens in an old barn, and an evening evangelistic service which all were expected to attend. The organizations looked after their own programme. I think we had some sort of impact amongst the young people because during the days we might be emptying the latrines and in the evening we were on the platform preaching. I suppose preachers who emptied latrines were quite something! I remember two of us emptying the buckets on one occasion and I slipped. The stuff splashed quite a bit over my fellow student who before his conversion had been quite a tough. He just gave me a smile!

Before I really handed everything over to God, one thing which had really worried me was my flaming temper. Every door in my old home had splits in the wood where I had hit them with my fists. Once when I was quite small they had pulled me off another boy when I was methodically banging his head on the pavement. I didn't always get the best end of an argument either, and this sudden rush of wild emotion had got me into plenty of trouble in the past. I rejoiced in the fact that in Christ I had found real peace from this demon. One summer we had a group of lads from some sort of Remand Home, in Birmingham. These boys let it be known that they weren't going to attend any religious service, but after a few days of sharing things they came around a bit in their attitude and said they'd come and hear what Christ had done for us. Just before that evening's meeting, a gang from the town was making trouble at the gate. Two of us were sent down to speak to them and ask them to go away. I suppose I was nervous about the evening meeting anyway, and when one of these young toughs moved to hit out at my companion all the old surge of rage came up and I bundled the attacker over the gate and the lot fled. I wished a hole would have opened up and let me crawl into it. I had let the Lord down very badly indeed. And how could I give a testimony about Christ's power to save when I had failed in this way? It was a very chastened man who gave a humble testimony to Christ's power to forgive that evening. I have tried to analyse this breakdown, but haven't really come up with a satisfactory answer except that I have to live near to Christ all the time.

Another summer I had had a number of calls on my time and faced going back to college without the necessary term's fees. This was a real test for me. As far as I can remember I told no one about this particular need — except God. I went up into that back bedroom in Tottenham and stated my case to the Lord, deciding at that point that I wasn't a C T Studd or Hudson Taylor and that my faith was weak indeed. A day or two later I received a cheque from a fellow student, which was enough to cover my fees. In his letter he stated that this was his tithe (that is, an amount which he was to use for God) and he had wanted to send it to a missionary society. However, as he prayed my name had come repeatedly to his mind. He still hesitated because of our close friendship; he was afraid such a gift might cause complications. But eventually he sent it, and it was the Lord's answer to my need.

After I had been in the college just over a year the educational authorities recognized it, which meant men applying to enter it could get a grant after they had done their national service. However, this recognition was not retrospective, so men who had done five, six or seven years in the services during the war received no grant from the government, while men coming in now after two years did receive a grant. I must admit to a degree of bitterness at that time, but I was greatly helped by another man's experience. Apparently he, too, had been resentful about this situation, and in a rebellious frame of mind had gone upstairs to his room. Almost from force of habit he lifted his Bible from the locker by his bed and opened it, and the words sprang out at him like fire, 'Hast thou lacked anything?' He dropped to his knees in a gesture of contrition and thanks. 'Nothing, Lord.' Not one of us failed to get through college through lack of funds. Not one thing had failed of all God's promises.

My last night at college I sat up late talking with a couple of old cronies. The Lord had done great things for us, whereof we were glad. I had come in very, very raw indeed. All Nations in those days pretty well accepted anybody and that was the only way I had got in. There had been times, especially at the beginning, when I had felt that all this was not for me. In a sense my studies had been done on my knees. More important than studies, I had learned lessons which I can only term as spiritual, and would probably need to learn again deeper down. The summer of 1949 was before me, and then the China

Inland Mission training home. I was an 'accepted candidate'.

I had to leave on an early train whilst men slept. I walked quickly and quietly into one or two rooms, grabbed a few pants, vests and shirts, took the armful down to the back lawn and strung them up between the two flag poles, then I wheeled my bicycle out of the shed, mounted it and cycled off down the road through Taplow to the A4.

4

THE BURDEN OF THE EAST

ONE OF BRASH'S lines was that God's call to service
and God's provision of the right life partner, in other
words the missus, were of equal importance. So he
had us all praying about our future brides. I took his
advice seriously and had at times prayed that God
would guide me along this line. Being of the nature I
was, I couldn't think that God had called me to be a
eunuch. At the same time the guidelines were
already laid down. She had to be a Christian, she
had to have a call to overseas work, she had to be
accepted for training with the CIM. This narrowed
down the field more than somewhat.

I cannot really believe that a few days after we
arrived at Highbury New Park, London N16, David
Bentley-Taylor had advised us to look round the
ladies at headquarters on the ground that once they
got to China and wore Chinese gowns they all looked
the same! Yet he must have said something along
that line otherwise I wouldn't have started looking, I
suppose. Anyway, I had a conviction that I should
wait until the spring term and then God would show
His plan, and accordingly got down to the business
in hand.

The buildings then belonging to the China Inland

Mission at Newington Green[1] were only the British headquarters of the Mission. One of the principles of the CIM was that the real headquarters were on the field in Shanghai, China, so that the mission was not ruled from an HQ miles from the field of battle, but from a place where the situation could be better understood. The job of the home office was to remit funds to the field, look after missionaries on furlough and arrange their rest, furlough studies and deputation programme, and interview and train prospective candidates. After an initial interview and some correspondence, candidates were invited for a year or more into the Training Homes. The ladies at that time were in a separate building from the men, although we had lectures together in a room in the basement at Newington Green.

To enter the CIM headquarters under the arch at the entrance was to go into a new world. Outside were familiar buses, fish and chips, the Star and the Evening Standard, cockney crying to cockney. Inside was the burden of the East. Hudson Taylor had been compelled, by the love of Christ and the thought of a million a month dying without Christ in inland China, to begin the China Inland Mission. He had put £10 into the bank in the name of the China Inland Mission after a crisis experience on the beach at Brighton in 1865. At that time he had already had several years in China, and returned to England in some respects broken in health and frustrated in

[1]These buildings became a hostel for overseas students in 1977, when the OMF moved to Sevenoaks

spirit. But God would not let him go. There in the board room at Newington Green, with its large oblong darkly-polished table, was the Bible Hudson Taylor had held that day at Brighton and in the margin of which he had written 'Prayed for ten willing, skilful workers'. I knew that you could be willing and foul the job up as well as the next man, and if you were not willing God didn't want you until you were. 'The Lord loveth a cheerful giver' is not confined to the financial sphere alone.

As you walked under the arch past the front buildings you saw the two Chinese inscriptions meaning 'Hitherto has the Lord helped us' and 'The Lord will provide', and above the door the simple words of Christ, 'Have Faith in God'. Inside the door and through yet another and you were in the prayer hall. Chairs were placed in three blocks and there was a small stage or pulpit with stairs leading from the main body of the prayer room. A huge map of China covered the wall to the left of the platform and on the right was a much polished brass plaque, containing the names of fifty or so martyred members of the CIM who had been murdered by the Boxers during the uprising of 1900. We candidates soon became familiar with what it had cost to bring the Gospel to inland China. You held your goods lightly, for bandits would take them maybe not once but several times; you were at times despised and rejected, regarded as offscouring; mothers buried their children, husbands buried their wives, wives buried their husbands, so that the Chinese could have the good news of Christ.

Yet there was nothing outwardly zealous about CIM people. I had enjoyed the noisy prayer meetings of All Nations, but in the CIM you prayed quietly and God also answered. The missionaries looked very ordinary until you talked with them. Then, unbeknown to them, you discovered their heroism and gentle faith. Sometimes I felt that I wanted to rush out of the building, collar the first person I could see and say something like, 'Do you see that building. Do you know what it stands for? It stands for the faithfulness of God! For eighty years God has kept hundreds of missionaries in China, moving them to live, love and die for Christ, supplying their needs, housing, food, travel expenses and something over, and all this without any appeal to the Church or the world, except for prayer for China.'

The Lisu of Yunnan, the Szechwan damp, the Kansu dust, the Lanchow Hospital, the Honan plain became commonplace to us candidates. Although we had never seen them they permeated us. During this year in training we were to learn the history, geography, religions and culture of China, the history of the Mission, a special document known as the P & P, and generally how to act in a way becoming to a China Inland missionary. We were given week-end assignments to various churches or mission halls and were under surveillance (not noticeably, but in an attempt to iron out a few creases). At the end of the training period we were interviewed by a council consisting of clergymen, professional men, missionaries and home staff.

There were five Britishers in training on the men's side that year, together with some others from the Continent. Maybe it was the fact that not too many men had been chasing degrees at universities in the past decade, or for some other reason, but we were a group with no degrees. We came from Scotland, Cumberland, Manchester, Liverpool I think, and Tottenham. I shared a room with a brother from Sweden. I cannot now recall how we communicated because he hadn't much English, but I know that we managed. We were brooded over by Mr David Bentley-Taylor, MA, who had been a missionary in Kansu, Northwest China. 'BT' was tall and handsome, dashing, visionary, enthusiastic and humble. He was one of the finest lecturers I have ever heard, and others with greater experience have remarked the same. He comes from old landed stock, or whatever they call it, and looks like it. He had been converted at Oxford University. He wasn't so much older than us bunch of old soldiers, but showed considerable experience in handling us. He could knock the self-satisfaction out of a man and still leave him smiling.

Fred Mitchell, a Bradford chemist, chairman of Keswick and scholar of the Puritans, man of prayer, somewhat august, was Home Director, and we had the benefit of his teaching. We also attended London Bible College, where Dr Kevan revealed to us the mysteries of the Doctrine of Grace. The Rev. Alan Stibbs, another first-rate evangelical scholar and lecturer, came from Oak Hill College to give us the benefit of his studies in First Peter. We certainly were in clover, getting the cream. No wonder when I went to Keswick a year later I found it a bit flat!

The Principles and Practice of the CIM, commonly known as the P and P, was the document which formed the constitution of the Mission. It had sentences like:

'Dr J Hudson Taylor, under a deep sense of China's urgent spiritual need and with an earnest desire to obey the command of Christ to preach the Gospel to every creature, founded the China Inland Mission in 1865.'

'The members of the Fellowship are compelled by the love of Christ and the hope of His coming to obey His command to preach the Gospel to all men and make disciples of all nations.'

'The direction of the Fellowship, under God, is the responsibility of the General Director.'

'Candidates must give evidence of maintaining a consistent standard of spiritual life and of trust in God.'

'Every member should recognize that his dependence for the supply of all Fellowship and personal needs is not on any human organization but upon God alone, Who called him and Whom he serves. Although funds might fail, or the Fellowship cease to exist, if the members put their trust in Him He will never fail nor disappoint them.'

'If the members are godly and wise, walking in the spirit of unity and love, they will not lack divine guidance in important matters and at critical times, but should another spirit prevail no rules could save the Mission nor would it be worth saving. The China Inland Mission must be a living body in fellowship with God or it will be of no further use and cannot continue.'

Each part was born out of some need and BT gave reason and anecdote for the inclusion of the item. Early on, as we sat at our desks in the lecture room, he made it clear that the CIM was not a perfect mission. We all smiled a little because we knew it was and he was being humble. 'If it were,' he continued with smiling face, 'how would you lot get into it?' We got the message. He gave us some of the inside story of the famed *Lammermuir* party which had sailed with Hudson Taylor as the first contingent of CIM for China. As he ran through the list it would seem that not one of those people should have been accepted! Finally he got to the last unfortunate target of his exposition on the P & P, 'and Miss Blank met a businessman and married out of the mission'. At that moment, in our zeal, we felt that that was the unforgivable sin! I am sure that every girl in the lecture room determined in that moment not to marry a businessman and thereby leave the mission!

By the end of the autumn term I was pretty sure that the CIM was the place for me. I felt that I was privileged in this. You can't spend seven years in the army with your ancestry being questioned by sundry NCOs without being suspicious of your seniors. Maybe it was my enthusiasm but I couldn't see a flaw in the administration at Newington Green. Their approach to life was punctual, considerate and progressive. They accepted me as a person. On more than one occasion my opinion was asked for by people who in every way were superior in character, intellect and spiritual understanding. This shook me. Some of these were clergymen. I had hangups on clergymen but was finding more and more what gems there were among them.

Then we began the spring term. First there was a thanksgiving service at which Mr Fred Mitchell spoke, and then 'BT' exhorted us to get together. That's when I saw her. I knew it was the one. My wife has always been secretly disappointed in me, I believe, because I was not first attracted to her because of the standard of her spiritual life. I admit without shame that she appealed first to me physically. I guess that is why God has made women like He has. The second thing was the way she glided across the room with a cup of tea in her hand.

Olga Rutherford was from Whitley Bay, a school teacher and the daughter of a professor of philosophy. Her father had been a Congregational minister but had left the ministry in his fifties before he married. Olga was certainly not encouraged to go to church. Mr Rutherford felt that education was the answer to man's need. He was a strong supporter of the Workers Educational Association and was a loved and revered figure in it. He died three years before Olga was converted.

At Cambridge Olga studied chemistry, played in the University hockey team and was a Communist. To Olga religion was the opiate of the masses; her father had been in the church but had come out of it; the salvation of the world lay in the salvation of society, and that through Marxism. At the same time she had a logical approach. If God existed, which He didn't, then what He had to say was of the utmost importance. Then she came into close contact with Helen Roseveare, a Christian. Helen said that Jesus Christ was a living reality to her. Helen was training to be a medic; Helen was not given to hallucinations; Helen could be right. This must be investigated. The argument and discussion went on for weeks, I'm told, and we know from Helen's side of it that her faith hung in balance. At a meeting held by Dr Barnhouse in a mission to the university he said, 'Some of you may not know what Christianity is all about, but if you have the slightest desire to do so please pray with me: "As best I know how I receive Christ as Saviour"'. Olga did, and her life was changed.

I was seeing this girl every day in the lecture room, but beyond the occasional formal greeting wasn't saying a word. There were reasons for this, primarily that we realized we couldn't play the fool with people's affections. When the women candidates approached the Mission they reckoned that in all probability they were putting marriage behind them. This was the sheer mathematics of the case: there were two women to every man in the CIM. To get through this tussle and then become involved in a friendship loaded with emotion, which later proved fruitless, would be grim indeed. Also at that time I had strong feelings about the value of the individual. People belong to their Maker; they are not for the use of others. It was important that I knew God was in this thing before I ever approached her. I had fallen hard, but then, I had fallen hard before; how was I to know the difference? I put out all sorts of Gideon's fleeces. This is a kind of Bible 'she loves me, she loves me not' but I couldn't think of anything better. I tried to work it a few times to cycle back with her from London Bible College, but she never seemed to be at the same lectures as I was.

All kinds of crazy situations occurred. She was keen on tennis and apart from one or two games in the local park in my teens, I'd never touched a tennis racket — that bourgeois sport ! I discovered some lessons on the basics in a magazine and decided to have a go. Four of us wandered over to the nets and paired off. I was pairing Olga. 'Should I stand up to the net?' she asked. 'Yes,' said I, not knowing what to say. I swung the racket for the first service and the ball hit her *clonk* in the back of the neck. She smiled sweetly, accepted my apology and moved two paces to the left. I swung again and hit exactly the same place. Double fault. Right in the neck. (Since then she always turns round when I serve.)

It was always difficult to reach these ladies, although now I cannot think why I didn't ring her up on the phone. That just wasn't done, and any-way, if she didn't answer the phone the person who did would presumably have put it around the place. Finally, one day in late April, I managed to meet her just as she was leaving the lecture hall. It sounds trad now and I suppose it was: 'May I see you this afternoon, Miss Rutherford?' So I told her the old old story and we moved on from there. Afterwards she said she hadn't had a clue what I wanted to see her about!

Things were looking bad in China. The disciplined, dedicated Communists under Mao Tse Tung were pushing down from the north, and we watched their progress on the map on the wall in the prayer room. Bishop Houghton, the General Director, gave us the text 'My heart is fixed, trusting the Lord'. We prayed for missionaries subject to all kinds of strains in China; we prayed for faith and courage for the Chinese Church; we praised God for testimonies of His faithfulness — but still the Red armies pressed down from the north. More and more CIM centres were engulfed in the advance. News became difficult to get. The order was given that CIM missionaries would remain with their churches and Chinese brethren; but in some cases this was neither practical nor advisable. Foreigners could be an embarrassment. In the face of tremendous odds 49 missionary candidates from seven countries had sailed to China just as we began our training. But now missionaries from China began to arrive in Newington Green. One day we were drinking tea, still dressed in tennis togs, when the Broomhalls arrived having left China by air just hours before. We felt embarrassed by our lack of participation but we could not share their agony. We could only pray.

In comparison with all the turmoil and suffering of China, the future of the Mission seemed almost irrelevant; but it was not so to us. Some felt that the CIM had finished its work; others were not so sure. We candidates knew nothing of the deliberations that were taking place, although we heard talk of a Bournemouth Conference. Mr Fred Mitchell, immersed in the purposes of God for the Mission, was a tower of strength. He called the eight of us who were finishing our training into his office. 'We cannot hold you,' he said with sympathy. 'We cannot tell the future. We do not know when and if China will open to the Gospel again. May God guide each one of you.'

I had no sense of panic or uncertainty. I was engaged to a Christian girl; God had guided thus far, He would continue to do so. He had supplied, He would provide.

At the end of that summer term we packed our bags and once again I was back in Tottenham. The text was still swinging from the old gas bracket. 'Thou art my God, early will I seek Thee.'

5
SIDEWAYS MOVE

I'VE HEARD IT said that God, in guiding people, sometime gets them moving in one direction in order to send them in another — something like going to Manchester from London via Bath! For nearly four years I had had this compulsion to train, to study, to work toward preaching the Gospel overseas. At first the outline had been fuzzy like a badly focused 35mm slide, but the outline had become clearer with the passing months — China, and the China Inland Mission. The goal had appeared almost in sight, the ball nearly in the net. Now China was definitely closed and the future of the CIM uncertain. Where do we go from here? Olga was staying on at the training home in Newington Green for another year, but what about me?

The compulsion remained but the doors I pushed wouldn't open. I talked to the Secretaries of several missionary societies; one man particularly, from a South American missionary group, was very kind. After a time of sharing and fellowship he said frankly, 'Brother, it's been grand to have this time together, but I see you have no call to serve with us'. And he was right. The Bible at this time said to me 'Wait thou only upon God'. I did a little forced ex-egesis with the Old Testament story of Ruth. There is a verse there which says 'Stay thou beside my maidens'. I reckoned that the CIM with its predominantly female strength was the 'my maidens' referred to, but I wasn't really banking my whole future on half a verse in Ruth!

So, with no other guidance, I decided I should get a job. Some people might have thought that this was going back on my call, but I didn't see it that way. I was fit and able to work. I went down to the Labour Exchange but the clerk couldn't weigh me up. I said I wanted a job in a factory but he kept trying to get me lined up with some sort of clerical job. I tried to explain to him that I wanted the kind of job I could leave suddenly without troubling anybody too much when God wanted me to move on. He looked at me a bit suspiciously, but got me a job in a small factory packing lampshades.

The man who was my mate on the job was a real shyster. He did as little as he could, but made sure he was around to open the boss's car door when the man arrived in the morning. It made me sick. I was working as unto the Lord and reckoned to do a day's work for a day's pay; that work did include doing a bit when the boss wasn't around but didn't include opening his car door for him. I figured he was strong enough to do that for himself. The news got around that I was a bit religious and was planning to be a missionary. At first there was some interest but nobody really wanted to make things personal where Christ was concerned. One day one of the men I hadn't had much to do with took the trouble to look me up during the lunch hour. His boy had some trouble with his foot and the man was worried that there was going to be permanent damage. I sympathized with him and then the whistle blew for work. I didn't see him for a few days, and when I did I asked him how the boy was. 'It's great,' he said, 'his ankle is getting well and things are going to be okay'. 'That's good,' said I, 'because I prayed for him', which I had. The man said 'I thought you would, that's why I told you'.

Then one evening after the Wednesday night prayer meeting the pastor of West Green Baptist approached me. 'Have you ever thought about taking a church, that is being a minister?' he asked. I certainly had not, and yet I cannot see now why I hadn't. In one sense it should require less qualifications to be a minister than to be a missionary. In Japan we are required to go into any area where there is no church and bring one into being, by the power of God, acting as its missionary, preacher and pastor until it reaches the place where it can call its own pastor. In England the situation is made to a degree, in the sense that believers and building are already in existence, although the future success or failure of the local church might well depend on the spiritual gifts and qualifications of the pastor.

Anyway, at that time I had not given the home-ministry a thought and had plenty of misgivings. Mr Stokes dealt with my objections and misgivings and put my name up to the area superintendents. God is in these things. The only man who showed any interest in me was in the southern area and I was invited to preach four Sundays at a small Baptist church in

Poole, Dorset. After the first Sunday I knew, and so apparently did they, that this was the place.

The active members of the church were few in number and mostly elderly, but they loved the Lord. They responded to the Word and I understood their faith — it was the same as mine. They couldn't afford much of a stipend, and as I was not an accredited minister of the Baptist Union they could not get financial help from that source. They found me a room in the district with a middle-aged couple who really looked after me, and offered me a stipend which would exactly cover my board and lodging and leave nothing over for clothes, travel or toothpaste. Still, I felt the Lord was in this and prayed about it. As a result the little group put the stipend up a little and I moved in.

The leader of the church at that time was an old man of nearly ninety. He had been in the YMCA in the days of D L Moody and really knew God in a personal way. He was nearly blind and could only just get himself along to church. I thought the first thing I'd have to do when I got to Poole would be to bury him, but he rallied for the winter and saw blessing in the church before God took him and the trumpets sounded on the other side.

Never having been a minister, I wondered how I should plan my days. I decided to spend the morning in prayer, Bible study and message preparation and reading. In the afternoons I would visit and most evenings I'd either be preaching or getting among the young people.

Just having come from Bible School, I hadn't too

much time for what I saw as 'frivolities'. Since I had been made a new man in Christ I hadn't been to see a film, or 'wasted time' in pleasures, and at first sight I wasn't too impressed by what I saw of the Christian Endeavour group. I'm glad I had the sense to wait a bit before I took any action. The group was practising a play for Christmas — I regarded plays as of the devil and felt what was needed was the Word to be preached. It was a play about a lad who loses his legs in an accident. His bitterness is increased by the fact that somebody buys him some roller skates for Christmas. In hospital he has a dream in which he approaches the manger in which the baby Jesus is lying, and watches the wise men and the shepherds bringing their gifts. He is ashamed because he has no gift to bring and is about to turn away when the baby reaches up and grasps his hands. In the last act the boy wakes up in the hospital ward shouting out, 'Jesus wants my hands'. I could see that the young people were being affected positively by the drama in which they were participating. Lots of people came to see it at Christmas and I realized that the Lord was using it.

Preaching on my first Sunday was an ordeal, in spite of the friendliness and encouragement of the believers. I chose as my subject 'The High Priestly Office of Christ'. Why I got involved in this I don't know, but I sure got bogged down in it. I suppose I preached from the Gospels in the evening. I went back to my digs feeling right down. I'd have to preach twice a week, as well as speak at the Bible study on Wednesday every week, and I'd run out of material already. At least that is how it seemed to me. I was glad to get alone with the Lord in prayer.

Because I found it good to have an objective in any study, I decided to take the Certificate of Religious Knowledge Bible Correspondence Course from the London Bible College. This would keep me moving, I knew. I began studies in Isaiah then which whetted my appetite, and I have been feasting on parts of Isaiah ever since. Some people say that the God of the Old Testament is a God of judgment, and try to make a difference between Old and New, but I cannot see it. 'I have nourished and brought up children and they have rebelled against me.' 'Come let us reason together, though your sins be as scarlet they shall be white as wool.' 'The Spirit of the Lord God is upon me because the Lord has anointed me to bring good tidings to the afflicted, He has sent me to bind up the brokenhearted, to proclaim liberty to the captives, and the opening of the prison to those that are bound.' 'Seek the Lord while He may be found, call upon Him while He is near, let the wicked forsake his way, and the unrighteous man his thoughts, let him return to the Lord, that He may have mercy on him, and to our God for He will abundantly pardon'. All these statements and many similar are voiced by Isaiah. And it's contemporary! A Japanese man picked up a copy of the Bible and read through Isaiah chapter five a few years ago. He asked me when these statements had been written and I told him, hundreds of years before Christ. He replied that this was a picture of Japanese society today. Presumably the remedy for those ills, that is Christ, remains the same.

After lunch most days I used to go visiting. I soon discovered that I needed to allow time for the older people to have a bit of a rest, so from around 2.30 I started out. The only thing I had to share with them was Christ, and in many cases they had had more experience of His mercy and presence than I had. I listened to them talk of what Christ meant to them, then I'd get the Word out and we'd pray together. Some of the young people in the CE were grand-children of these old ones, so we prayed for them. One or two of the old folks had lost their other halves. They had no doubt that the husband or wife who had gone before would be there on the other side, not for any merits in them, but because of Christ's salvation. I believed this too.

One elderly lady had lost a son in his middle twenties. He had had a science degree and was, he had said, an atheist. She asked me if I thought her boy was in heaven. I didn't answer directly but a few weeks later she told me this story. She hadn't been too happy about her minister visiting the boy when he had been sick so she asked another pastor to, and whenever this second pastor came the boy seemed encouraged and strengthened. Just a few days before he died he said to his mother, 'Who's that standing in the corner?' She said, 'There is no one there'. The boy replied, 'It's all right, I have the living water now'. I listened to this story and a little while later told her that I had every reason to believe her boy was indeed with Christ. She asked me why I thought so, and I asked her if she knew what was meant by her son's allusion to the living water. She replied that she didn't, so I showed her Christ's promise in John 4 — 'Whosoever shall drink of that water I will give him shall never thirst; the water that I shall give him will become in him a spring of water welling up to eternal life.'

I am pretty sure now that the twenty or so teenagers coming to the church would never have taken my message if they hadn't been softened up a bit first by the social activities like table tennis, the play they worked on for Christmas and so on. I spent a lot of time with them; I was always at their club activities fooling around with them up to a point. Most of them were High Schoolers in their final years and studying for exams. I realized that I couldn't help them in their studies, I could only offer them Christ; and this is what I did.

As we got into the programme, Sunday was a full day for me. I used to go back to my digs for a big Sunday dinner, but spend the rest of the day down in the small room at the back of the church. I took a Bible study from three to four, and then I got down to prayer and study of the Word for my evening message. There was a tradition in the church that you gave a message for believers in the morning and an appeal to the unsaved in the evening. I wanted to come into that pulpit Sunday evenings with a message from God if at all possible. It had to be, nothing else could meet the need.

Congregations began to build up. Twenty-five, thirty to forty in the mornings. Forty, sixty, seventy in the evenings. Hardly revival yet. I was concerned for the youngsters. Years later a girl who was converted at that time told me that I held them over the pit in those days. I was aghast at the suggestion. The thing that gripped me then and does today is the grace of God — His mercy, His love — and this is what I thought I had been preaching. Maybe the Holy Spirit showed her the meanness of her heart in refusing God's grace. She is certainly a very happy woman in her faith today.

I have never been able to call for decisions for Christ easily. Maybe it is pride on my part, but I think it is rather that, as I came to Christ in the quietness of my own room after a long period of Bible reading and teaching, I expect others to do the same. Anyway, after I had been in Poole a few months I began to feel that I should make what is called an 'altar call' in the Salvation Army. I prayed about this and wrote to my pastor at West Green asking his feelings, and he replied that he was praying for me. So one Sunday evening at the end of the message I asked for those who wanted to give their lives to Christ to come to the front of the church. As we got up to sing the last hymn I could see that old Mr Pilgrim was mouthing prayers, his eyes closed and his face reflecting glory. A young man pushed his way in front of two others and began coming forward, so did another, then some of the girls — five, six, seven, eight of them, standing there determined to make their testimony to Christ. Praise the Lord! He had honoured His Word. We closed with the benediction and I talked with them as a group and made arrangements to see them all separately. I could not contain my joy.

We arranged baptismal classes and made plans for the service. The baptismal pool under the floor-boards in front of the pulpit had not been opened for nine years. When we opened it up it looked like it! But we needed no pushing to get it cleaned up. We discovered that there was only one way down into the pool. This meant that the four girls would be baptized first and then would go round to the small room at the back which could be divided by partitions. Then the four lads would follow.

It was the first baptismal service at which I had ever officiated, and I was quite nervous. But it was a wonderful service. The little church was packed with about 150 people, and to these dear old folk who had held the testimony alive through many lean years, this was harvest indeed. One by one the teenagers came forward. As they came into the pool, each gave a simple statement of why they had believed and then as the crowd sang 'O happy day' they were immersed and brought out, buried with Christ and risen with Him, too.

On Monday night I went round to see the Church Secretary. He was a grand chap, a blunt Welshman who had fought in World War I. That night his face was glum. 'The treasurer wants to resign,' he told me. The treasurer was a retired engineer, converted many years previously at an open-air meeting in the USA. He wasn't really used to Baptist ways, but the church was near and he had enjoyed evangelical preaching and the Wednesday night prayer meeting. However, something had apparently upset him at the baptismal service and now he wanted to quit. I didn't know what to do, so I did nothing as I knew he would have to give me my monthly cheque that week. When he arrived I was alone in my digs and invited him in. He came and sat down heavily. Handing me my envelope he said, 'This is the last I'll be giving you'. 'Oh,' said I, 'am I getting fired?' 'Certainly not,' said he, 'but I'll not be coming any more'. Then it came out. The gist of the problem was that he had been the helper designated to put a towel round the first boy who came out of the pool. Somehow he had not been told about the arrangements and was quite upset for a moment because he couldn't see where the boy was to go. Someone soon saw his plight and assured him that the partition was in place in the back room, so it was quite in order to continue round into it. He felt that he had been made a fool of. He had been on tenterhooks anyway because he hadn't seen a baptismal service before.

'I made a few mistakes on Sunday too,' I said, and told him how one lady had said to me as the congregation came out of the church, 'If I had had to give a talk about my faith before being baptized forty years ago, I would never have been baptized. You have no right to subject those young people to such a strain.' That put me in my place. Several other people had gone by shaking hands and then a man said, 'You haven't baptized these young men and women correctly. Instead of giving their full names you only gave them their first names.' I thought back and he was absolutely right. I'd got so used to calling them by their first names that I hadn't used surnames. I was also hauled over the coals about something else which I had done wrong. This was all very good for me, and kept me in my place.

I wasn't looking for sympathy and the treasurer knew it. 'You know, sir,' I said, 'the devil doesn't like baptismal services'. His reply was spontaneous. 'That is just what my wife said.' 'How about if we have some prayer,' I suggested, and we got down on our knees together and told the Lord about it. Nothing more was said about resignation.

I was beginning to be pulled in two directions: I had been approached about taking the Baptist Union exams. I hadn't anything against it, but what about my call overseas? Olga in London was still of that mind. And then we began to get letters again from the China Inland Mission.

6
JAPAN CALLING

THE MAIN POINT of the correspondence was whether or not we would consider going to Japan.

With the atom bomb assault on Hiroshima and Nagasaki and the surrender of the Japanese forces, the cult of the divinity of the Japanese Emperor had been proved false and the Japanese were in a state of stupor. There was a spiritual vacuum. General MacArthur, as early as 1946, had made an appeal for two thousand missionaries, and there were accounts of thousands turning to Christ. It was a reaping time.

As far as the CIM was concerned, what should have been curtains had been shown to be only Act I. Around the beginning of 1951 while missionaries were still pouring out of China, many living in Nissen huts on the hillsides of Hong Kong waiting for a passage home, the General Director of the Mission held a conference with the other directors in Australia. From the conference came a cable to all home departments, 'Lengthen cords, strengthen stakes. While emphasising priority prayer for China, conference unanimously convinced Mission should explore unmet needs preparatory to entering new fields from Thailand to Japan. Haggai 2.5'

This was no more than the first Christians had

done — when persecuted in Jerusalem they spread out and preached the Word everywhere. However, there were some doubts where Japan was concerned. For a start, many of the missionaries had seen awful acts of barbarity perpetrated on their Chinese brethren. It wasn't easy to forgive. Also some felt that preaching the Gospel in Japan, while being known in China, might perhaps bring reaction from the government against Christians in China. Still, there had been unmistakable signs of the Lord's leading at that conference in Australia, and so Japan was included in the vision of a new CIM, now called the Overseas Missionary Fellowship.

One eminent Japanese pastor and evangelist has suggested that God has given Japan three opportunities to accept Christ. (This does not include the period over four hundred years ago when Roman Catholicism made great advances in the country and was then ruthlessly stamped out.) The first Protestant advance or wave came during the latter half of the nineteenth century. For two and a half centuries the country had been closed to foreigners, under a dictatorship, the Shogunate, which ruled with an iron hand. But eventually the Japanese people realized that the power of the western nations could not be denied and the Shogunate was challenged by radical forces under a group of talented young men. Fighting led to victory which put the Emperor back into his place of power. These new leaders of the nation led emissaries to the western world. They learned military tactics from the Germans, naval know-how from the British, law from the French and agriculture and business methods from the Americans. For some time there was still no real freedom for Christianity but some doors were opened. For example, the Japanese asked for lecturers for new colleges, and these lecturers, mostly from the United States, were Christians and taught the Bible to the students.

With the change in the dynasty had come the abolition of the barons of the old feudal system, which resulted in thousands of *Samurai* being without employment. These young men of culture and of pride had been trained in military arts and it had been their work to protect their barons and, if necessary, give their lives without question for their feudal lords. Now many of them were sent to college to acquire the new learning, and there they also learned the Bible and the Holy Spirit worked in their hearts. These students were wonderfully open to Christ as Lord, and bands of them from the colleges went nationwide preaching the Word. Some were disowned by their families, some embraced poverty, some faced ridicule and persecution; but nothing could stop them. As missionaries came in, the intellectuals of Japan saw immediately the superiority of the teaching about One God over against the Shinto pantheon of gods and the poverty of the Buddhism of that period. A missionary writing home before the turn of the century was able to say, 'I do not think missionaries are needed in Japan and within six years Japan will surely be Christian'.

That must have been the peak of the first wave. What went wrong? There was a dual counter-attack.

Teaching came into Japan which denied the authority of the Bible, the deity of Christ, the natural sinfulness of man, the resurrection of Christ and His coming again. This teaching commended itself to many of the Christian leaders in Japan because of its philosophical ideas, and the message of the power of Jesus to save through His blood began to be regarded as unnecessary. At the same time the government of Japan saw the need for a unifying factor in their state philosophy, to build the Japanese into a united people. For this the political leaders went back to Shinto, which means literally 'the way of the gods'. The high priest is the Japanese Emperor, and every Japanese town and village has its Shinto shrine. Now there was to be State Shinto and religious Shinto. Religious Shinto was for personal combating of bad luck brought by evil spirits, for lucky charms, for the purification of buildings, and for new year worship customs, weddings, and so on. State Shinto, however, was to do with the unification of the country under one ruler. The Imperial Rescript on Education aimed to use education to unify the country. Although it was claimed that this policy would not interfere with other religions, in fact it weakened the testimony of the Christians who did not stand firm against it. By contrast the Korean Church, in the face of severe persecution from their Japanese masters, refused to accept the edicts of the Japanese government.

The second wave of God's grace came into the situation through Japan's rapid industrialization. At that time thousands of young people were leaving the security of their homes on the farms for the loneliness and snares of the big cities. In the early years of this century they slaved and laboured in city factories and workshops, living in hostels and doss-houses. Into this industrial upheaval came God's messengers, particularly those from the Holiness denominations. This partly overlapped with the first wave which was still represented by such scholars as Dr Uchimura Kanzo who in the 1920s was having Bible studies for great crowds in Tokyo. At the same time the Salvation Army, the Japan Evangelistic Band, the Oriental Missionary Society and the men and women brought to Christ through the preaching of these organizations reached out to the industrial workers of the new Japan. Yamamuro Gumpei, the leading Japanese Salvationist of the time, led his Christian forces physically, tearing down the barricades behind which hundreds of young girls were kept as prostitutes. Dr Kagawa, a famous Christian socialist, was reaching down into the slums of Kobe; his books on slum problems are still relevant today. The mission hall of the JEB in Kobe was packed night after night with tired young people who heard the message of hope through Christ, sanctification by His Holy Spirit, the power of God to heal and the soon-coming return of Jesus Christ. There were programmes to take Christian literature to every home, every farmhouse, every factory throughout Japan.

In the early 1920s a terrible earthquake and fire devastated large areas of Tokyo. Thousands died in the holocaust, trapped in the flames between the rivers. Stories are told of Christian evangelists who stood up where the fire was raging, urging people to turn to Christ. When one was overcome by the flames and fell, another took his place. So the Church grew.

Again there was a dual counter-attack. Japan's war plans included effective control of the Church; Christians were regarded as dangerous for they were people of independent ideas who had rejected the basic concept of the divinity of the Japanese Emperor. Christians were outside the total community, holding allegiance to an authority other than the Emperor. Control of the Church was gained through a law that appeared to offer benefits to the Church. The government promised three things — official recognition of Christianity, the right to own property and exemption from taxation on property. However, by refusing to recognize as a religious organization groups of fewer than fifty churches and five thousand members, the government pressured churches to unite and thus gained effective control.

In return for the dainty morsel of recognition, the Church surrendered both its liberty and faith. The Ministry of Education held the power to decide what the Church could believe and what it could teach. No creed which referred to God as creator of the world was acceptable to the authorities since this conflicted with Shinto myths, and no reference must be made to God as judge of all the earth, since this implied an authority higher than that of the Emperor.

The other blow to all-out evangelism came somewhere about 1928. A hitherto fiery Japanese bishop,

renowned for his devotion to Christ and his sacrificial zeal, came out with some new teaching on
Christ's return. He said to hundreds of his
denomination that all evangelism should now cease.
All Christians should now wait for the return of
Christ which would be quite soon, probably when
the Japanese Army reached Jerusalem. It was now
the duty of Christians to pray for the peace of
Jerusalem but not to proclaim the Gospel. This command effectively stifled that outgoing group of
Christians.

As the militarists grew in power in Japan, some
were very interested in a prophecy which said the
Japanese Army would get as far west as Jerusalem,
and the military police began to make inquiries.
'And what is going to happen when the Imperial
Army reaches Jerusalem?' they asked as they inter-
rogated these pastors.

'Christ will come again,' was the answer.

'And what then?'

'Every knee shall bow.'

'What, even the Emperor's?' they taunted.

'Yes,' replied the doughty followers of the true
and living God.

That is how a number of them found themselves
imprisoned for Christ's sake.

I heard of a commotion in a state prison in the
north of Japan in the war years. Prisoners asked for
an interview with the prison governor as they had a
complaint to make. Three of these bedraggled
shaven-headed unfortunates were marched into the
prison office and made to bow low before the gov-

ernor; the guards watched them carefully, ready to beat them over the head for any insubordination. The spokesman spluttered that a man in the jail was getting preferential treatment — he was getting better food than the rest of the prisoners. The governor asked who it was, as such a thing was impossible in a prison like his, which was run strictly on democratic lines. 'That Christian pastor is getting better food. He must be, because every time his bowl is filled he clasps his hands together and fervently thanks God for His gracious provision.' The convicts could not see that any man would praise God for the kind of rice soup the prisoners were given! The governor had them kicked out of his office, assuring them that it was the pastor's faith which was different, not the daily gruel.

The third opportunity which God gave to Japan to accept Christ was the post-war period, with the country once more open to the preaching of the Gospel, and it was this wave which Olga and I were to be involved in.

Olga and I had our private problems. We hadn't thought it right to marry during this time of uncertainty. But the CIM at that time had a rule that new missionaries could not marry for two years after arriving in the Far East. This was to give the woman as well as the man the chance to learn the language thoroughly and really get involved with the people, for in the CIM it is reckoned that both man and wife are missionaries. Now that the possibility of going overseas had become a probability again for us, a two-year wait seemed a long, long time, especially as it was decided that Olga should not leave until six months after me.

Another difficulty was that we had no particular interest in going to Japan. We had been completely China-orientated, and all I'd heard of Japan was Mount Fuji, cherry blossoms and geisha girls. I knew about the attack on Pearl Harbour and the atrocities, of course, but four years after World War II I couldn't get too churned up about these. We'd settled the debt with Hiroshima, anyway. (This wasn't a particularly Christian reaction, but I was trying to think objectively about guidance at that stage.)

Our biggest problem, however, was the whole question of going in with the Gospel under Western guns. To us there was something wrong in this unholy alliance between Western power and the Gospel of peace. It was the fashion then, and still is, to point out how missionaries and the armed power of the West went together. This isn't strictly true; it can also be shown that Christian missionaries have been against the opium trade, the slave trade and other vested interests. Still, we didn't want our path made easy by the physical victory which had been won in the Far East.

It didn't help that Olga was London and I in Poole. Our letters kept crossing and for a while we got nowhere. We knew that God was calling us overseas; my early careless approach to the call, 'I'm not doing anything else, so I may as well have a bash at this,' had been replaced by a pressure I dared not turn my back on. We knew that God was calling us into fellowship with the CIM, and we had waited while the Mission untangled itself after the withdrawal from China. Now the call to Japan had come. Isaiah 50.10 says, 'Who is among you that feareth the Lord, that obeyeth the voice of his servant, that walketh in darkness and hath no light? Let him trust in the Name of the Lord and stay upon his God.' The voice of the servant of the Lord in this case was Mr Fred Mitchell, Home Director of the CIM. Finally it seemed right to accept his request.

And yet the Lord was definitely blessing the church in Poole. I was concerned about the children in the district. The Sunday School was quite small and we couldn't really handle many more children, because we had neither accommodation nor teaching staff. Still, I felt we ought to try something and suggested a week's campaign to be called 'Sunshine Corner'. The deacons weren't too sure about this because they had never tried anything like it before. I was sure some of the young people in the church would give a hand, and promised that if the church members would give hospitality to five friends of mine they would trust God to meet the rest of their expenses. At the same time I wrote to five of the people who had been with me at All Nations and CIM (one of whom was Olga, of course), asking them to pray about whether they should come.

We had a great time with Sunshine Corner. The church hall was pretty full every day for a week, with children singing choruses, listening to the stories, memorizing Bible verses and learning of the love of God in Christ. I learned a couple of lessons along the way, too. One member of the team was staying with a very gracious and friendly couple, whom I had often visited but never prayed with because I didn't want to embarrass them. However, on his first morning there Eric said to them, 'Come on, we'll read the Bible and have prayers, then your daughter and I'll do the washing up.' This couple were not embarrassed but thrilled to bits.

A friend with whom I used to do open-air preaching wanted to meet Olga, so I took her and another girl along to have dinner with him and his wife in a smart restaurant. As we came out, they went one way, and we said our goodbyes and turned to go the other. Then I heard the man call me; he came running up to me, said 'I want to help these two girls' and pushed some notes into my hands. I never knew him do anything like that before or after, and finance had not been mentioned during the meal. When I passed the money on to the girls June, Olga's friend, was obviously quite excited. I understood why when she said that she had had the fare down to Poole but not the fare back, but still had thought that she should come. We also discovered that Olga, who had thought she was in the black, was actually running a small overdraft because of a cheque which had not been recorded.

After my second Christmas at Longfleet the decision had to be made, and we knew there was no valid reason why we should say no to the CIM and Japan. I went back home to Tottenham for a few days to arrange packing, passport, vaccinations, inoculations and the rest. I was booked on the P & O boat *Chusan*, on its maiden voyage to the Far East, and given a conglomeration of labels to stick on the baggage, all four boxes of it. Things were really moving.

Gordon Welch, CIM's Deputation Secretary, came to Longfleet for a farewell service. He said that they couldn't all go to the Far East to preach the Gospel but they could stand behind me in prayer. I felt very humbled that I could share with men like him and the rest at Newington Green in the work of preaching Christ.

It was really after we went to Japan that we had the gradual confirmation that we were in the will of God. After we arrived in the Land of the Rising Sun I felt a need for a real love for the people such as Christ has for us all. By this I do not mean a sentimental emotion that goes into hysterics over the culture or the politeness or the festivals, but a steady affection which would burn and be real even when I saw the worst in people. We prayed about this, and also asked a group of people at home to ask God for it for me.

The steam locomotives of Japan in those days had centre aisles, and people sat in couples opposite one another. I was travelling somewhere, studying Japanese and occasionally glancing through the window of the train out over the ricefields and the farmhouses to the purple mountains beyond. Across the aisle from me were four men, labouring types wearing puttee trousers and sandals dividing the big toe from the rest of the toes. Their teeth showed fully as they grinned. They were smoking, playing cards and drinking saké, the Japanese rice wine. A couple of them already looked flushed.

An American soldier with a .38 automatic strapped to his belt walked through the carriage and disappeared through the sliding door at the far end. The card-playing fraternity paused from their recreation to observe this phenomenon, and it became apparent to me that it was the gun which offended them. They began to joke about it. 'I suppose his mother told him to wear it.' 'Maybe he doesn't know the war has been over for ten years.' At first it was all pleasant and the normal kind of banter that you would expect, but one man began to get very angry and wanted to know how much longer they had got to have foreign soldiers toting guns around their country.

At this point he suddenly noticed me, and as he squinted in my direction he realized that here was a foreigner, a *gaijin*, to whom he could address the question. He lurched over across the aisle and squatted over against me with a bump. Then he peered for a few seconds at my face and leaned forward. With his face about a hand's breadth from me, his breath smelling of liquor, he shouted 'I hate Americans!' I pointed out quietly that I was an Englishman. This stopped him for a moment and he leaned back. Then a new thought hit him and he leaned forward again and shouted, 'I hate Englishmen!' By this time the passengers in the carriage were very quiet and embarrassed at his un-Japanese behaviour. I put my hand on his shoulder and replied, 'I love the Japanese'. All the adrenalin seemed to go. He grinned sheepishly, wagged a finger at me and stated emphatically, 'You are a Christian, aren't you?' With the steam taken out of the encounter we were able to talk and everybody else relaxed, and soon he was back with his card-playing brethren, but not before urging me to visit him in his home. At the same time he asked me not to tell his children about Jesus, for they were all Buddhists in the family. It was not until I reached my home that I realized with sudden joy how the love of Christ and the prayers of friends had brought bad-tempered me through that incident.

7
BACK TO SCHOOL

I SAILED FROM HONG KONG to Yokohama on a 9,000-ton Scandinavian banana boat. There must have been other passengers, but I only remember Mr and Mrs Reynolds, en route for Japan with the CIM as I was, and their two boys David and Timothy. The weather was fine when we left the harbour, making our way down past Kowloon and out into the open sea. But then it grew dark, and later we ran into heavy seas and we were into a typhoon. The ship with its engines racing would labour to the top of a tremendous crest, teeter there with its screw clear of the water while its deck shuddered then, nose down, it would go pell-mell down the other side. It always amazed me that it didn't keep going right down to the bottom, but after taking on a bit of water it would get its nose up and climb up to the top of the next one, only to repeat the operation. Some passengers, including Arthur and Joy Reynolds, were seasick and confined to their bunks, but David and Timothy were very lively indeed and I spent my time during the typhoon watching that they didn't go overboard.

By the time we reached Taiwan we were clear of the typhoon and out into calm seas and blue skies again. The new government of Taiwan was suspicious of English people at that time and wouldn't allow us ashore, so we spent the time watching the bales of bananas being unloaded from the ship onto the wharf.

Mr and Mrs Reynolds were very friendly and helpful, but with their two little boys to occupy them they hadn't too much time to give to me. So I found myself a nook right in the bow of the ship from which I could look for Japan. I saw its mountains first — a purple haze against the blue of the sky. In these cosmopolitan days you can meet every nation under the sun in almost any big city of the world, but in those days people mostly kept themselves to themselves and stayed in their own countries. I had never yet met a Japanese.

One morning I woke early. The ship was strangely quiet. On board ship you get used to the continual hum of the engines, so that when they stop the silence hits the eardrums. I looked out through the porthole and there was Mount Fuji, a pale mist-like cone on the horizon. Japan at last! During the day the boat edged into the side of the wharf, and I looked down and thought that the navy was out in force — a little way back from the wharf were crowds of people wearing sailor collars. I discovered later that they were Japanese high school girls! All Japanese school children from the age of six to fifteen wear uniforms. It has changed a bit, but the old uniform for the girls was a black skirt or slacks and this sailor-like jumper. The boys had a navy blue outfit and hat rather like the uniform of the soldiers in the American Civil War. Some would feel that this is regimentation, but it helps the Japanese. They are a shame-conscious people and it is difficult for them to be different, so girls and boys, rich or poor, wear the same uniform.

We were met at the wharf and, having seen our hand baggage through Customs and ourselves through Immigration, got on the train for Karui-zawa. It is quite warm in Tokyo in May, and all the windows on the train were open. Japan hadn't recovered from its war-time damage, and the old train seats were hard and threadbare. The train was crowded with men and women, some of the men in their underclothes, the women in baggy blue trousers and jumpers, many with white headscarves, and all carrying enormous bundles. These are going out of fashion a bit now, but the Japanese had a custom of carrying things around in a *furoshiki*, or large square handkerchief with intricate and interesting designs, such as a white stork or crane, or the pine and bamboo. With it they will wrap up a small present to take to a friend or acquaintance when they visit. They will also use larger *furoshiki* to wrap up their bedding and to move from house to house. Most of the parcels that these Japanese in the train were carrying probably contained black-market rice. I never did quite discover why they did this because there was plenty of rice, but the Japanese still had rationing, and as the farmers could meet the ration quotas easily they supplemented their income by doing a certain amount of black-market trade. Maybe it was the Japanese approach to encouraging private enterprise!

We travelled between rice fields for miles, and then the track ascended very sharply, as mountains do in Japan. This particular section of track was interesting as, because of its steepness, it had a special kind of ratchet which was attached to the engine, and the train climbed up in that way. The rhythm of the thing was one of my earliest impressions of the country.

Japan is very hot in the summer and anyone who can gets up into the mountains; Karuizawa is a favourite summer resort. There used to be three ghetto-like groups in Karuizawa: the missionary community, the foreign diplomatic community, and wealthy Japanese. The missionaries hold conferences in the summer, and some missionaries have their own accommodation, wooden structures with high ceiling, arm chairs made of bamboo and afternoon tea at 3.30.

A few years after World War II, Karuizawa was invaded by hundreds of young missionaries mainly from the United States. Living in the summer houses among the pine trees, they spent their time doing language study or making forays into the populated towns and villages on the Tokyo plain to preach the Gospel.

OMF rented a big house, which from the air must have looked something like a London Transport sign. There was a central dining room, a wide airy place suitable for summer but freezing in the winter. From the dining room there was a corridor with a number of small rooms leading off it, and exactly opposite on the other side of the circle was another corridor. The community consisted of 17 to 18 single ladies, three married couples, David Hayman and me. All the single ladies kept very carefully to one corridor, and Dave and I were well chaperoned by the three missionary couples between us and the dining room.

Dave Hayman was from Australia. His parents had been missionaries with the CIM in China and his father was one of the men who had been captured by the Communists on their famous Long March from the south of China to the north in 1935. Mr Hayman had spent months in captivity but had finally been released. David himself had been one of a party of schoolboys who had been captured by Chinese pirates. He was a somewhat taciturn man and not given to publicity, so to help conversation along I used to suggest to new arrivals that they might like to hear from David about the time he was captured by pirates. He didn't always appreciate it!

We lived in a small room at the end of the corridor. He had a bunk, a desk and a chair, and I had a bunk, a desk and a chair. We were given our language study material and began to get on with it.

Up to the time of my arrival, I had not given much thought, if any, to language study. There are exceptions, but it is pretty well true to say that if anybody is going to be a missionary at all, he will have to get the language of the people among whom he will be working. For the Westerner getting Japanese, it is a fascinating but formidable task. At that time the Japanese mostly believed that a foreigner would never learn Japanese anyway. So the attitude of the teacher often was, 'Well, if he can learn a few sentences that will be about as much as he can handle. A few may even be able to preach, but certainly none will ever be able to read or write the Japanese language.' Things have changed, and we now expect new arrivals to speak, read, write and understand Japanese in two to three years. That doesn't mean that they don't go on learning it for the rest of their natural lives!

Japanese has two sets of 51 sounds in its alphabet, written to about two thousand Chinese characters, which were brought to Japan in the fifth century AD along with Buddhism. The Chinese use one character to express an idea and usually the character has one sound. The Japanese work on a system of permutations, using two characters to express a thought, and very often the sounds are different. In this way you get some startling mix-ups. The story is told of a missionary who was preaching on the love of God for mankind. Now the word for mankind is *ningen* — the *nin* is the character for men, and the *gen* is another character giving the idea of humanity. Unfortunately he got his vocabulary mixed up and he was preaching using the word *ninjin*. The sound *jin* can also mean 'man' just to make things more confused. *Ninjin* means carrots, so he was telling the Japanese audience that God loves carrots! The Japanese are a well-trained people and know how to behave, and so they listened impassively to his eloquent and fervent address. The next morning, however, three of the Japanese presented the missionary with three long, clean carrots.

I ran into similar language trouble after I had left language school and was preaching in the north of Japan. It was a spring evening at the time of the cherry blossom festival. Crowds of farmers had come into a park-like area and were drinking *saké* (Japanese rice-wine), and enjoying the view. When I stood up to preach there must have been a hundred or a hundred and fifty farmers standing around, and I wanted to impress upon them the fact that men's hearts are basically evil. One old gentleman, however, insisted that he was 76 years of age and his heart was as good as it had ever been. The Japanese have two words for heart, one meaning the seat of the emotions and the other the physical heart. I had only learned the word for the physical heart, and thought that covered the whole thing. So I was telling this group that every man there had a weak or poor heart. From then on the conversation got more and more confusing as far as I was concerned.

The Japanese language is class-orientated — the older superior speaking to the younger inferior, the man speaking to the woman, teacher talking to pupil, are all distinguished by different kinds of speech, different kinds of verb endings and polite forms. Grammatically they put everything in front of the noun, then say the noun and follow it up with a verb. As I watched Japanese people speaking on some occasions, I used to wonder why the listener had such an impassive face, and I came to the conclusion that he was waiting for the verb. Until the verb arrived he didn't know whether the man had eaten or was going to eat, would not eat, didn't like to eat, or what he was talking about. He needed that verb to make the whole position clear.

In many ways David Hayman was what I wasn't. He had always been a straight, upright sort of person, captain of the old Chefoo School in China, University graduate, army officer — yet we were soon friends, sharing our thoughts from the Word and praying together, especially burdened to get the Gospel out to people around us. On one occasion a director from our Headquarters in Singapore visited us, and David waxed really eloquent on the wonderful fellowship that he and I, although poles apart in so many ways, were having in Christ. This director, who had spent many years in the East and was probably more eastern than western, went for a long walk round that old building in Karuizawa and then came back and looked at David and said, 'David, what is the trouble between you and Doug Abrahams?' He just couldn't believe that things could be that good!

Today we talk about culture shock, and of course there is such a thing but I look at it from another angle: the Bible tells us that there is a personal devil. We read about the devil in Genesis and get another picture of him in Job, and our Lord Jesus Christ had quite a time with him while He was on earth. We are told that the Son of God was manifested to destroy the works of the devil. It doesn't matter how inefficient or futile or weak a Christian may be, it is the devil's job to confound him, fool him and defeat him. If someone is called to go abroad to preach the Gospel, then the devil's objective is to bring him down. When our Lord received the confirmation at

His baptism that He was indeed the Son of God, this was followed directly by a fierce spiritual conflict, and all those temptations came along the line of the voice that He had heard confirming His Sonship.

It was my own experience, and I am convinced as I look at other missionaries new to the work that it is theirs too, that Satan attempts more in that first year or so of acclimatization in a foreign country than ever after. There were a number of things which threatened to bring me down during that time, and the first was on, if you like, the domestic front. I was already 32, and wasn't born to be a eunuch. I had somehow got it into my mind that the Mission might allow us to get married after one year on the field. But after I arrived in Japan they told me quite clearly that I would have to wait the full two years, which was the rule then. It was a good rule in a way. The OMF tries to identify with the people among whom we are working, and as near as possible we live in the style they do. Our whole purpose in being in this land is to lead them to Christ. If the missionary wife doesn't have this kind of desire, then things may not go too well. But if she has a sense of call, then she must get the language. Unless you learn the language you can't communicate — it is essential to be able to speak it. That's the main reason for the two-year rule — to give the wife as much opportunity for language study as her husband and to avoid, on top of every other acclimatization, adjustment to early married life and the possibility of children. I knew all these good reasons in my head, but it didn't help one bit in my spiritual struggle.

Perfectly rational reasonings cannot always help the emotions. I hardly avoided the root of bitterness springing up.

Another attack came along the line of cross-cultural adaptation. The only Americans I had met before I came to Japan were GIs in the US Army, and now here in Karuizawa I was in close daily contact with American brothers and sisters in Christ. We differed in the way we talked, the way we ate, the way we thought and the way we worked. Most of the young Americans there at the time were fiercely fundamentalist. Anyone who didn't quite agree with them was a modernist, if not apostate. (I ought to say that this was a purely local and temporary situation and was probably exaggerated by my own reactions.) Still, these missionaries from the USA really loved the Lord and had a sacrificial outlook. They had cars, refrigerators and all the rest of the equipment, but their homes were wide open to the Japanese people. The Englishman tended to think of himself as part of a team, whereas as far as he could see the American was fearfully individualistic. I think maybe I resented too their very openness and generosity. Whatever it was, the devil tried to exploit the situation and again I had to battle through to victory, and subsequently to a real fellowship with many of my American brethren, which has continued over the years, and I trust is mutual. It is amazing how much of our Christianity is associated with our own culture and cultural patterns. It doesn't really matter if a man slurps when he drinks his soup as the Japanese do, or wears his hair long or

short or whatever, as long as he loves the Lord and
His Word.

In England I had been fully occupied in Christian
ministry, preaching, preparing of messages, coun-
selling, leading Bible studies and prayer meetings,
visiting, doing young people's work, the lot. Here in
Japan I was suddenly being treated like a schoolboy
(that's what it felt like, anyway), doing language
study with the teachers two hours a day, and by
myself for another six. I was completely unable to
talk in any depth with the Japanese people around
me, and as a result I experienced moments of depression. There were times when I wondered if I would
ever get the language, and prayed desperately that
the Lord would give it to me so that I could preach
His grace and love to this people.

Up on the plateau around Karuizawa, we were
pretty well isolated from the Japanese people anyway. From it, many of our American friends loaded
up their cars with tracts and loudspeaker equipment
and dashed round the villages and towns preaching
the Word and distributing literature. Some might
have thought that a lot of this was superficial —
maybe it was, but some were converted and testify to
those days as the time of their salvation.

We are all creatures of our own environment and
background. The leaders of the Mission, and this
included our Superintendent in Japan, had been in
some desperate situations in China. They had seen
the highly disciplined idealistic Communist army
over-run the forces of the Kuo min tang. They had
seen experienced Christians of many years' standing,

brothers in Christ, accusing one another; it appeared that the work of decades had suddenly been swept away. Our Japan Field Superintendent, Leonard Street, had been responsible for part of an area of N W China when he had been forced to leave the country, while others were still under house arrest there. It is not surprising if his thoughts and prayers at that time were more in China than they were in Japan. Yet time does not stand still, and the Mission had to move on, and make new policies and plans. These were bound to be affected by what had gone on in China. Perhaps many of the leaders felt there were only a few years or even months before the rest of Asia went Communist. It was not the time for long-range, carefully-laid-out plans, but rather a time to get out and preach and teach the Word, raising up small groups of believers as quickly as possible. It was felt that from the beginning there should be no financial help to any national worker. This wasn't because the Mission was too tight-fisted, but rather to give the principle of faith full play in the hearts of the Christian nationals. We didn't appreciate all the problems that this principle was going to bring us in future years.

We missionaries were flooding into Japan, and each group was as it were planting a stake or taking an area in which to start its new work. Where was OMF to go? There was prayer and discussion; the pioneer spirit of the old CIM and maybe even the fact that the Superintendent had worked in far off N W China, caused us to look on the farthest fields. There were areas in northern Honshu and in

Hokkaido where there were only churches in the larger towns, so it was felt that Aomori Province and Hokkaido were the places in which we should work. The first missionaries who went northward were people who had already done a couple of years of Chinese language study before having to leave China. Now after a further fifteen months Japanese language study they finally headed north, going to small towns in Hokkaido where there was no witness for Christ — to the town of Mori just inland, and the fishing towns along the Hidaka Coast out from Tomakomai.

Hokkaido is an interesting place. Winter is arctic; the winds come across from Siberia from just about Christmas time, bringing the snow, and after that it is a struggle with severe winter conditions. July and August are hot — well up in the eighties. The best time in Hokkaido is autumn when the mornings are fresh, the evenings are cool and the skies are blue. Hokkaido literally means 'north sea road'. Up until the mid nineteenth century it had more or less been left to the Ainu, a primitive people smaller than the Japanese and much more hairy, who had their own religion and their own culture. (This is now fast dying out.) Meanwhile the Japanese people, ruled by the Tokugawa family since the seventeenth century, had been living in isolation, forbidden to leave their native land and with hardly any foreigners allowed into the country. In this isolation Japan's national characteristics were formed. But some of the rulers were aware of the trends in the world. They saw the great powers carving up China, and the ships of the

American fleet, Perry's black ships, began to make their presence felt in Japanese waters. Finally in 1868, in what is known as the Meiji Restoration, the Tokugawa Government was thrown out and a new government, more directly linked with the Emperor, sent his emissaries throughout the world to bring back western culture, western knowledge and knowledge of western arms. To give the fierce two-sworded *Samurai*, knights of the old barons and unemployed in the new situation, something to do to keep them out of trouble, the new government sent them north to Hokkaido. There was a two-fold purpose in this; to make a shield in case of any attempt at takeover by the Russians, and to keep the *Samurai* from any ideas of rebellion themselves. Up until then *Samurai* had been soldiers and had not worked with their hands, but at that time they became farming stock, each being given a piece of land and told to go build a house and till the soil and grow food. It was a tough pioneer situation.

For nearly eighteen months, David Hayman and I and the rest of the new OMF members struggled with the Japanese language. We used a course that had been printed for the use of army personnel. (It had quite a useful vocabulary, if in parts it wasn't too useful for some of our lady missionaries!) We struggled with the vocabulary, and I think I managed to get through some of the examinations, though not others. At last the day came for our designation. Leonard Street called David and me into his little office and talked around generally for a bit. Then he said, 'I would like you to begin a work in

Kutchan'.

There is a story in Ainu folklore that a defeated tribe badly mauled by its enemies packed its belongings, its spears, its knives and its small amount of clothing, and began a long trek into the mountains. Further and further they went away from their enemies, and higher and higher, until finally they came out onto a level plain at the foot of a great mountain now called Mt Yotei. The chief said, 'Here we have our tools and here we shall have peace,' and this is exactly what the characters of the name Kutchan mean.

Kutchan is high in the mountains at the foot of a yet higher one, on a plateau well away from outside interference. The Superintendent had tried to find us some kind of accommodation in Kutchan itself, but try as he might, there was no house to rent. This isn't surprising really when the custom at that time among the Japanese was to rent as little as possible. The laws were all loaded against the house owner, so nobody was very happy to rent, let alone to a foreigner who might not be around to pay his rent. We finally found a disused DDT factory just outside the town in a place called Rokugo. The factory was all burnt and broken down but the old office remained, and with the use of some plyboard we were able to fit up a room upstairs to sleep in and another room downstairs to live in.

When we had got ourselves settled in we began to look round for a language teacher, which was essential because our eighteen months or so of language study hadn't got us very far along the road.

One big-wig in the town offered to teach us, but his teaching seemed to consist mainly in coming along and saying to us in English 'It is a very fine day'. We weren't quite sure how you fired a man who was a big-wig in the town, but we managed it somehow. Next we were introduced to the local fire brigade chief who offered to teach us, and he showed all kinds of hidden talent.

Dave and I had been learning the language together and we hadn't had too many problems. Now we were working together as a team, trying to reach the people in the town round about, and it was interesting how mixed up we got because we both tried to follow each other. If he did some language study, then I felt I should do some language study; but he could keep going longer than I could. Frustrated, I would get a bundle of tracts and maybe a Christian book or two, and go out down the street to find somebody to talk to. Then he would feel bad about studying the language when I wasn't, so he would get up from his language study and go and look for somebody to talk to as well. Even in those days I liked a bit of a sleep just after dinner, but as soon as we had finished our bowl of rice or noodles, Dave would come upstairs, get out his language books and start studying. I'd come upstairs and feel bad about getting on my bed, so I would begin studying too. When I looked over my shoulder, there he would be fast asleep. By this time I had got over my desire to sleep and there wasn't much I could do about it anyway. You wouldn't think these things were very important, but it's significant how the seeds of problems come out of this kind of thing. Anyway, we recognized the old enemy and eventually found a good basis for work.

We had been told by all kinds of people that the Japanese didn't like having their language murdered, and we began to get sensitive about this. One day a Japanese Christian working with the Christian Literature Crusade visited us. He had been a soldier during the war and had escaped death by the skin of his teeth. We were talking to him about evangelism, and asked when he thought we should start street preaching, thinking in terms of six weeks or two or three months ahead. 'What's the time now?' he asked. 'It's about 11.30,' we said. 'Well,' he said, 'let's gather at half past twelve'. So off we went with him for our first street preaching. We wrote a couple of texts out on a piece of paper and had these hidden in our hands. At least we could shout out the text, and then we would say a few words about it, and speak the text again, and a few people would come along and we would talk to them. The Lord spoke to us in those days about the reality of death, and the urgency of the Gospel.

I played my mouth organ with the window wide open and the kids would come along to see this strange long-nosed foreigner. Pretty soon we had a bit of a meeting in the house with twenty or thirty of these kids. Dave and I hadn't much language, but we acted the parts. I can see him now trying to look like an elephant when in build he is more like a giraffe. The kids would get a great laugh out of it, and they would get some teaching at the same time.

We knew they were getting the message because late one night there was a real banging on our front door. Dave and I came down and opened it, and in came a man, drunk as a lord, and was he mad! He stamped around and cursed us and said to us, 'Who is this person who has been telling my child there is only one True God?' We tried all ways to get him quietened down, but he wouldn't, and kept on insisting that he was an officer of the Old Imperial Japanese Army, letting us know in no uncertain terms. Finally I shouted 'Shut up!' in a loud voice, and he became quite subdued. For my part I was upset that I had spoken to him in such a way. He finally stumbled out of the house, ripping his trousers on our post as he went. It was sad because the following day when he passed us in the street, he was too embarrassed to answer our greetings; he never did become friendly.

We invited the children to bring their parents along to see some slides of the life of Christ and other Bible stories. We had quite a crowd of parents in and halfway through the film-show one of the children was sick. The mother was quite embarrassed; she cleaned up the mess, picked up the kid and went home. The next morning I thought I would call to see how the child was. The mother with a smile said, 'He has died'. This really rocked me and I could hardly believe it, but it was true. The child was gone. We learned from his mother that he used to say the Lord's Prayer which we had taught him.

8
LIFE IN KUTCHAN

GETTING A HAIR CUT in Japan is not a simple matter; it is a ritual. Instead of taking ten minutes it takes 45 minutes to an hour. The client sits solemnly in the chair while a boy brings hot towels and the hairdresser selects one, wraps it round the head of the client and folds it. He then presses on various parts of the head and brushes up and down vigorously. When the head and hair are wet, the towel is removed. Next the hairdresser takes quite a time selecting the right parting. He will view it from various angles and if you happen to be a tall man and he is a short man, he has a little difficulty looking from above. Then he starts off with his electric clippers, followed by hand clippers, then scissors and finally thinning scissors. The next ritual is the shaving of the forehead and the back of the neck. The barber attacks the leather strap fiercely, sharpening the open blade. A piece of paper is selected and laid on your shoulders. Hot water is poured into the shaving basin and a thin lather made up. Finally, after shampoo, there is a vigorous massage in which you are not sure whether or no your head is going to be removed from your shoulders. All this can drive some men who are in a hurry out of their minds, but most people are completely relaxed by this ritual.

Dave and I got to know the local barber quite well. He had a family business, with his wife coming in to help when he was busy, and his twenty-year-old son giving a hand to clean up when he was home from university. This boy was the local ski champion and a gymnast. David had spoken to him once or twice about the Lord, but the lad was highly amused. He held the firm conviction, as do many Japanese, that that sort of religious stuff is for old people or those who are sick. 'I don't need it yet,' he said. 'One of these days maybe, if something happens to me, I'll give it some thought, but not at the moment, thanks very much.' In spite of this he was quite friendly.

We dropped into the shop on one occasion to pass the time of day, and asked the man how his son was. He replied that his son wouldn't be coming home any more; he was dead. This really shook us, and we asked how it had happened. The father told us that when the boy went back to university he was living in a lodging house, and he and his friend bought some canned food. The friend only ate a little, but his son had eaten quite a lot. There was some poisoning in the food and the boy was dead within an hour. The father seemed to be quite cheerful about the whole matter, and we didn't quite know what to say. We learned later that the Japanese hate to show any grief in front of anybody, for this causes the hearer grief as well.

I think these two deaths, the small boy and the barber's son, did a lot to waken David and me once more to the urgency of spreading the Gospel. Our problem was how to do it. We still hadn't too much language. We could prepare simple messages by using a lot of Bible verses and getting the hearers to read these themselves. We had also memorized a few 'religious' sentences — simple lessons in Japanese explaining the way of salvation and the need for it. Still, if we had a question pushed at us, most of the time we couldn't understand what the questioner was asking. At that time we usually spent the mornings in language study and the afternoons out trying to meet people. Most Japanese then were too shy to invite foreigners into their homes, and although we often invited men to drop in on us, they seldom did so. If we saw a group of men working on a construction site or in the fields, we would go up and talk to them and give them Christian literature, and then we would go round the town and leave Christian literature at the homes we visited.

I was in the town one day and to my amazement, instead of the usual handful of people on the streets, the whole area was crowded with farmers dressed in their best clothes, women in kimono, dark-suited high school boys and girls in pleated skirts and brightly dressed children. Sideshows and stalls selling fruit and souvenirs had been set up on the sidewalks. It was the local town festival! I rushed back home to call David and collected all the tracts we had with our name and address on them, went back into the town and started giving them out. While we were doing this a young high school boy came up to us and asked us if we were Christian missionaries. We said that we were, and he said he was interested, so we invited him back to our house.

This was the beginning of a friendship with Doki-san, eldest son of a family in the dry cleaning business. Gradually, one or two began to drop in for a Sunday morning meeting until at times we had half a dozen or maybe even ten, but the person who was most interested was Doki-san. All through that winter the two of us did our best to teach him the contents of the Bible. We missionaries were all for the simplicity of the Gospel, and felt that anything which was not in the Bible should have no place in the perfect church which we were about to form. We had long discussions about the rights and wrongs of the ordained ministry and other things connected with it. A week or so before Christmas, Doki-san asked if we were going to do anything for the children over Christmas. Were we going to have a Christmas party for them? Dave and I looked very solemn and explained to him that there was nothing in the Bible at all about Christmas as such; it is not even known whether December 25th is the birthday of Christ anyway. He listened to us talk for about twenty minutes, and at the end of it he said, 'Well, if you are not going to buy the children any oranges, then I'll have to do something about it'. Needless to say, we had a children's party!

The pastor of a church about forty miles away had invited us across for their Christmas Eve meeting. It was snowing. There were only 25–30 believers there, but each one had an impressive faith. After the candle-light service there was a supper — not too much food around, but each one had a few Japanese rice cakes and green tea. I just felt the love of the

Lord and the fellowship of His people was right there. When Dave and I got back we decided that maybe we should have a Christmas party too. We had contact with half a dozen young farmers in the district, an old man who lived across the way, and the members of our English high school Bible class. We got them all together into our room all bowing very stiffly, starchily and formally, and began with a few party games. It took a long while to get going because every game had to be described in minute detail — the Japanese hate to make mistakes. However, our old gentleman friend was determined to keep up his dignity and he did very well sitting there solemnly in his chair. Finally he thawed out and the party began to go with a swing. We finished up with some carols and a brief explanation of what Christmas is all about. As one of the young farmers went out he said, 'I never though that it was possible to enjoy yourself without getting drunk'. I too had learned something — that there was another way of preaching the Gospel.

One Sunday afternoon when we stepped out into the street we noticed that the wind was getting up a bit. It wasn't the normal kind of wind which comes along in gusts; it was just a continuous pushing. We noticed that people across the road were putting up their heavy *amado* — a kind of wooden sliding partition which they normally put up at night. We asked what the trouble was and they told us a typhoon was on the way. Typhoons start to form somewhere down south of the Philippines from June/July onwards, come up with increasing force across Hong

Kong and Taiwan, and then usually hit the south of Japan and work their way up the coast or inland bringing heavy rains, strong wind and destruction. The simple wooden houses of the period could not take much of a battering. Still, by the time typhoons reached Hokkaido, they had usually blown themselves out and were officially listed as 'strong winds'. On this particular Sunday the wind was more than just a gale. We not only put up our *amado* but were putting heavy boxes against the *amado* so that it wouldn't bend in with the force of the wind. When I slid open our front door and stepped out, I thought there was also an earthquake, for the whole ground was heaving beneath my feet. Then I discovered that it was the roots of the big tree across the way, which was being blown down in the wind. Then the heavy rain came in great sheets, drumming on the roof, so that it was only by shouting that we were able to make ourselves heard. The big barn just behind our house was beginning to lose its roof, and we could see the sheets of metal bending upwards as the wind got under them. Men were struggling to tie the whole thing down with ropes, and David and I went across to help them, heads down against the wind. David was well up on the roof trying to adjust the rope when we heard a crash behind us, and turned just in time to see the roof of our two-storey house nicely deposited in the street. Our possessions were soaked and some were useless.

That night the *Toya Maru*, the ferry which runs between Aomori and Hakodate, went down with the biggest loss of life since the *Titanic*. There had been long discussions as to whether it should leave Hako-date harbour, but somebody made the fatal decision and the ferry started off for Aomori. It didn't even get outside the bay, for it was blown inshore and the keel hit the shallow bottom. The chains which were holding down the railway carriages in the hold broke, they all slid to one side and the vessel turned turtle. Very few passengers survived. On that vessel was an old Methodist missionary, who had a lifebelt. A young high school boy next to him, who was fran-tic with fear, did not have one. The old preacher pulled off his lifebelt and gave it to the boy, and said to him 'Remember this, lad. Jesus said "I am the Resurrection and the Life"'. They recovered the old missionary's body from the sea a day or so later.

That same night too, some distance away in the town of Iwanai, an old paraffin-burning stove was knocked over. In seconds the house was alight, and in that crowded area the flames spread in moments. Two-thirds of the town became a raging holocaust. Mr Seki, our language teacher and chief of the local fire brigade, was among those who dashed across country to help in fighting the fire. Because his fire engine was smaller than the others, he was able to get into a narrow road and there use his hoses to ad-vantage; and that is where the fire was stopped. David and I grabbed some clothes and other things and went across to see what we could do to help, but we felt strangely out of place. All you could see of two-thirds of the town was red earth and a few burnt metal saucepans and kettles. Yet already the Japa-nese were beginning to pick themselves up after the disaster.

You can't live with a man closely without learning all sorts of things about him. One of the discussions Dave and I used to have was on the question of time. Was it right to do things like domestic chores ourselves, or should we employ somebody to come in and do them for us? Doing them ourselves would mean giving time to that instead of to language study and getting the Gospel out, and employing someone was to an extent helping the local economy. On the other hand, we didn't feel right employing people. We had a long discussion about the stove. It was a wood-burning stove on the second floor, so we had to lug the wood up from downstairs and we had piles of it around the place. There was a long metal stove-pipe outside the house which was poked through the wall at a T-junction and came into the house several feet and down again into the stove. Dave felt that we ought to clean this ourselves. I said that it was a professional job and that if we started doing it something would go wrong. However, we eventually decided to do it ourselves. We asked Doki-san about it, and he told us there was a special kind of brush, a very long one with a flexible bamboo handle. I got up on a chair and took the end junction cap off the pipe, then gingerly removed the pipe from its piece outside and tilted it at an angle without realizing what I was doing. A steady flow of thick black oily soot descended gently onto David's best suit, in fact his only suit. As well as his suit, everything else was covered with a thin layer of black soot — our blankets, books, desks, in fact the lot. Dave's reaction was that of a Christian gentleman. After that we got the professional in to clean the stove.

Catering for ourselves was a bit of a problem too. Neither of us was an expert cook, and there wasn't too much to buy. We could get a tin of bully beef, or eggs which tasted more like fish, or a slab of greasy pork. I had brought two cups and saucers and two plates and two knives and forks with me from England, but David hadn't got anything. We bought some cheap Japanese teacups from a local shop and built up a reservoir of jam jars. Before the winter came, cooking was a problem. The method used in the country places then was to cook on a charcoal burner, a round earthenware affair with a tiny grate and a little grill across. We would fan the coals outside the door early in the morning, trying to get this charcoal alight. We were seldom successful and what the people around thought of us, I don't know: for a Japanese man to do such a thing was completely out of culture. They must have felt sorry for us, because they started bringing across hot burning charcoal in little shovels and emptying it into our charcoal burner. This certainly saved us time, even if we lost face. Then it was suggested that we ought to have an old lady come in and help us. We couldn't communicate too much, but she knew we needed something to eat at midday and would cook us bowls of noodles or some rice dish. One day she was talking to me and our conversation went like this:

'I don't think Mr Hayman likes Japanese food.'

'Oh, I'm sure he does. Why do you think he doesn't like Japanese food?'

'Well, we Japanese, we like to make a noise, we

like to slurp when we eat food that tastes good, but he doesn't make any noise.'

It was obvious from this conversation that I did make some noise, so I must be acceptable. I mentioned this to David and afterwards he tried his best, but he never really managed it. During our meal times we might burst into a few verses of a hymn, or get up and look at the map on the wall, or start a conversation, which again was outside the Japanese culture pattern, for in Japan in those days you ate your food as quickly as possible in silence and then got back on to the job. One day the old lady mentioned this to me too. I explained to her that not all foreigners ate the way we did, and that some people were quite civilized.

Every so often either David or I went off to the big city of Sapporo to have a weekend with Mr and Mrs Street who had moved up to that city. During this weekend, which was a highlight in our existence, Mrs Street fed us up in good style. David was starting off one morning from the house for the mile walk to the station, and I was upstairs. I just called out to him, 'Cheerio, David!' and he replied and off he went. When I came down the old lady said to me, 'Aren't you going up to the station to see him off?' I said, 'No, he'll be back again on Monday, you know'. 'Oh, in Japan we don't do that. If somebody is going on a journey then we go to the station and see them off.' And this is true. At every railway station, for every passenger who is getting on the train there must be five or six, or even twenty or thirty people standing around waiting to see them off.

Japan National Railways does a good business in
platform tickets!

In every Japanese town there are a number of
public bath houses. As you go into the men's section
you take your shoes off and then step up to an open
space, with glass doors through which you can see
the men having their bath. After undressing and
dropping all your clothes into the bamboo basket
provided, you step into the bathroom itself. In the
communal bath there are a number of taps with hot
and cold water. The body is swished down completely with hot water (or cold if you prefer it but
there aren't many who do) and then you step right
into the bath and squat down up to your neck. I am
sure if we had hot water like this in our English baths
we would never get into them, but somehow, by getting right into it you are able to do this. You sit still
and pretty soon the perspiration comes out on your
forehead. This is really relaxing. Then you climb out
and wash the whole body down, this time with soap.
To see a Japanese do it is amazing — he scrubs,
polishes and rubs assiduously, getting rid of every
last possible piece of dirt. If you have a friend in the
bath house, he'll come and scrub your back for you,
and then you can do his. You have really arrived in
the Japanese culture then. Then more hot water into
the handbasin provided, and throw it all over yourself, trying to avoid the person sitting right next to
you doing the same thing, and then back into the
bath again for another period of perhaps five minutes. The body heat itself dries the body, and all that
is needed for the whole operation is a very small

hand towel. When David and I went for our first bath, the locals were amazed. Most of Kutchan had never seen a foreigner anyway, and a foreigner who was prepared to get in the same hot water that they were getting into was a real sight for sore eyes. They were obviously pleased and flattered. When Mr Seki saw us the following morning, it was obvious that the story had got around.

'So you went to the public bath house last night,' he said.

'Yes,' we said. 'We were dirty.'

Oh,' he said, 'that's real democracy, isn't it. I didn't think that foreigners would get in the same water that we get into.'

* * * * *

The snow began to fall in Kutchan about the end of November. It fell silently and continuously in great white flakes, and soon farmers from the outlying farms were coming in on their horse-drawn sleighs and working to keep the snow off the railway lines, carting it away to dump outside the city. David dug down into his boxes and came up with a brand new, good quality leather overcoat made in Australia. He put this on and sauntered out into the street. Two hours later he was back.

'I don't want this overcoat,' he said.

'What's wrong with it?'

'Oh, nothing's wrong with it. It's just that men keep coming up to me and touching it all the time.'

'What do they say?' I asked.

'They say "What a good quality overcoat," and I see them shivering in their thin cotton coats. I don't think I want to wear it any more.'

'Righto,' I said, 'I'll wear it.' So he gave it to me. I wore it on three or four occasions then I came back to David and said, 'I've had enough'.

'What are you going to do with it?'

'Let's give it away.'

'Who shall we give it away to?'

Before the snow came we had gone on what David called a walkabout, up into the mountains giving out tracts and talking to farmers and others, and we had come across a very poverty-stricken place. At first we thought it was a haystack, then we saw the smoke coming through the roof and when we got near it we realized that there was a family inside. Outside was a girl trying to cook some potatoes, her eyes red with soot. In Japan only those who are really poor eat potatoes, even though Kutchan was a potato growing area.

'Do you remember that family?' I said to Dave.

'Yes, I remember them, but I don't know that we'd find them now that the snow is falling.' We wrapped up the coat anyway and decided we'd try, and struck off across the hills. We were soon more than knee-deep in the snow, fighting our way through. We had just about given up hope when we saw the smoke rising from the valley. There, sure enough, was the place. We trudged down the hillside and handed over the coat. The man looked scared to death and so did his family. I think he must have wondered what these two foreigners were about. We didn't know what to say, so we just walked away. I often wonder what he thought and what he did with the coat.

It was after this that the police called on us and asked us not to wander off the roads during the winter, saying it would be difficult to explain to the government what had happened to us if we got lost. The snowfall in Kutchan is one of the heaviest in the country, and after a time you are digging your way out of your house, and up snow steps onto the path. In the main street, when the street lamps were not so tall as they are now, you could bang your toe against one of them if you were walking on the road, and you could look down into the second floor rooms in the houses as you went by. Little kids, well wrapped up and looking more like snowballs than anything else, ski from the tops of the houses into the streets on tiny little skis about two feet long.

When you got up in the mornings you looked out onto a silver and white world. Pretty soon farmers would come on their sleighs and the road would be messed up with horses' manure, but then it would be covered again and you were all right until the next day. When April came with the thaw, all the manure and other trash in the roads was revealed, so that you walked in mud and muck up to town. The Japanese believe that basically a person is neutral when he is born; he is neither good nor bad, but he picks up the dust of the earth as he travels through it. Every year they have a purification festival in which all the evils and wrong actions of the past year can be blown away. I used to use an illustration from the

Kutchan snow, saying that we cannot do away that easily with our wrong actions; before God they are sin, and although we may cover them up at the time, in the day of reckoning all these things will be revealed and we will see the whole of our actions throughout our life before Him. There is only one covering, and that is the covering of the precious blood of Christ. This illustration really seemed to get through to the Japanese, and I hoped it would help them to see their need for Christ's forgiveness.

In Karuizawa we used to play volleyball as exercise after a day's language study, and during one game I fell awkwardly and twisted something in my knee. I had thought the pain would go off, and it did for a bit, but then it came back again. For months in Kutchan I was limping around with a little pain, though I didn't like to say too much about it. Finally I decided that I had had enough, and the doctor sent me down to Tokyo for an X-ray and then an operation. I was down there for about a month all told, two weeks in the hospital and then two weeks sitting around. When they opened the knee up, they found some congealed blood, and part of the bone seemed to be diseased, so they cut that away. I came back to Kutchan with my knee in plaster, and really needed som physiotherapy but couldn't quite see how this was possible. Then I discovered a man in the village who had an interesting electrical treatment. His equipment consisted of batteries and a couple of wires with metal plates, and he would apply one side of the metal plate to one side of the knee and the other plate to the other side, and send an electric shock through the knee. I would sit for about half an hour at a time under this mild electric treatment. I never knew whether it did any good or not, but it slowed me down quite a bit.

9
JUST MARRIED

OUR WEDDING in the Christian Centre in Sapporo was an international and interdenominational affair. The preacher was a Canadian Presbyterian; the organist was the wife of an American Lutheran Brethren minister; an Australian took the photographs; two Japanese and two Americans made up a singing quartet; and among the ninety guests were fourteen nationalities. The organ was a small harmonium, one leg of which apparently broke half way through the wedding march and had to be held up by a missionary while the organist pumped furiously. Leonard Street, our Field Superintendent, gave the bride away, and the Americans experienced culture shock when they saw that the wedding breakfast was a real meal. I gather that Americans have a drink and a slice of cake at wedding receptions. For the wedding to be legal we had to travel down to Yokohama to the British Consul. Nowadays planes travel half-hourly between Sapporo and Tokyo, but in those days it was a 26-hour journey by train. For that period we were married before God but not before the British Government; we spent the night on the train sitting up. We nearly missed the train anyway — waiting at Sapporo station we couldn't understand why nobody was moving until one of our Japanese friends dashed up and told us we were in the wrong queue. A very startled bride and bridegroom dashed past an even more startled ticket collector, followed by a crowd of excited Japanese and foreigners with bits of our baggage.

The marriage at the Consulate had an air of authority: it may have been the consul himself, or it may have been the pictures of the Queen and Winston Churchill, and the Union Jack over the table. We came out of the consulate into the cool December sunshine, facing the traffic of the Yokohama streets. It was then that I made what Olga considers was my first basic error in married life. Someone had very kindly loaned us a house for a few days in Karuizawa, but we had two weeks to spare before we went north again. We hadn't been able to make any arrangements before because we hadn't enough money. People had asked where we were going for our honeymoon and had regarded our silence as secretive; but our silence was economic. However, the generosity of friends at the wedding had changed all this, and now we had some money to spend! Olga turned to me outside the consulate and said, 'Where are we going?' I replied, 'To the Japan Travel Bureau'.

'Where is it?' said Olga.

'Straight down this road,' I replied. I had been to JTB once before in Yokohama and figured I knew where it was. 'Just trust me', I said.

We walked for about ten minutes. Olga said, 'How much farther is it?'

'Not much farther.' We walked for another ten

minutes.

'Hadn't you better ask somebody?' said Olga.

'No, it'll be all right,' I replied. Finally I asked somebody! The man pointed back toward the consulate.

'You'll find it just the other side there,' he said. A man should always be very sure of his ground from the first day of his married life. It was a good honeymoon anyway.

We were looking forward now to working for the Lord together, and we had been designated to Shizunai. To get there we had to travel by train north from Tokyo for about fourteen hours to get to Aomori, which is right at the end of the sausage-shaped island of Honshu, and then you take a ferry four and a half hours across the Tsugaru Straits. Although it is only a short trip it can get really rough! Then the train goes right round in a kind of bow shape through to Tomakomai which is a big city, after which most people go on to Sapporo. Olga and I got off the express train at Tomakomai, alighting from the comfortable express onto a cold crowded platform. There opposite us was a little train, snorting with impatience. It looked solid enough on the outside, perhaps a little dirty and a little old. Olga said it reminded her of the drawings that Emmett used to do in *Punch*, those ridiculous-looking wobbly engines which pulled equally queer passengers to their destinations. We rushed across the platform with the throng and pushed our way toward the carriage door, clambering into the already-crowded train with our cases and parcels to add to the confusion. I don't think I have ever seen an empty train in Japan, unless it was at a siding. This one was no exception.

The custom in those days was to put your parcels on the seat while you stood up. I have never seen a small boy or girl offer a seat to an older person in all my time in this country; this is probably because of the crowds on the train, as any child would be suffocated in the crush. So the order of priority is: parcels on the seat, then if there is still any room left, little children on the seat, then if there is still any room left, adult men sitting down. The way of carrying a parcel is first to wrap it up in a *furoshiki*, a large coloured handkerchief from the size of a headsquare up to the size of a bedsheet. The two opposite corners are tied together across the parcel with the other two left undone, and the whole parcel is heaved onto your shoulders. The two spare ends are then tied across under your chin, with the cloth of the *furoshiki* covering your shoulders. Anyone standing too near a person carrying a load like this is liable to be sent flying if the person turns round suddenly to talk to someone.

The atmosphere in the train was friendly. Tradesmen and women were returning home, their day's work accomplished, and a feeling of wellbeing prevailed. Women in long baggy trousers rested their legs on their large empty packs. Men were sprawled out over the seats. The aisles were littered with packs and people. We picked our way through them to two empty seats. Opposite us was a coal-burning stove with its chimney going through the roof of the train. A weary traveller snored contentedly with feet outstretched on the stove. The guard edged slowly along the compartment. We were ready with our tickets. He stopped opposite us, shovel in one hand and coal scuttle in the other; he stoked up the fire. The stove door clanged shut and on he trundled to the next stove. Strange smells cut the air. Even empty packs betrayed the trade of the fishmongers. Some of the passengers were enjoying chewing dried cuttle fish. The air was thick with tobacco smoke. Suddenly we got a new rich smell and a startled growl from the gentleman with his feet on the stove — the refuelled stove was a little warmer then the comfortable footstool he had used before falling asleep! Undaunted, he produced from a large coloured handkerchief an old piece of fish and placed it on the stove. When it was sizzling hot he ate it. Hungry as we were, the combination of fried fish oil and baked woollen stocking completely robbed us of any appetite that we had.

The train continued to snake out along the coast. The sand is grey with volcanic ash, and the greyness of sea on our right reflects the greyness of the sky. On the left the country is flat right away inland: mostly grassland, the grass bending in the stiff breeze, a horse or two looking over a fence, scattered farm houses and silos. After a bit the terrain changes and we find ourselves running along a narrow ledge, the sea within a few feet of us and a steep cliff on the other side. Here the coastline improves and autumn reds, greens and yellows stand out vividly against the clear blue of sea and sky.

I decided to try out my Japanese and turned to the square-looking man beside me. There is a standing joke about asking if you have seen somebody, for example, 'Have you seen Mr Tanaka?' (*Tanaka* is the equivalent of *Smith* in England.) 'What does Mr Tanaka look like?' 'Oh, he is on the short side, dark hair, dark eyes and has a wide smile.' This is how all Japanese looked to me when I first arrived in the country. Now I wonder why I ever thought that way. Every Japanese is different in size, shape and facial features, and yet there is something which makes him a Japanese. He is not Chinese and he is not a Korean. The man I decided to talk to was typical — a farmer with heavy boots and riding breeches and a grey hunting coat. I passed the time of day with him. He was very surprised that I was able to speak some Japanese, and as usual complimented me on it. A few sentences later he couldn't understand my questions and I couldn't understand him and things got a bit confused. (This happens sometimes, as when Olga asked a lady the way to the post office and the lady very kindly led her to the ladies' room.) Nevertheless, talking to this man was a useful way of passing the time, and with patience we managed some communication.

The train was stopping and starting about every ten or fifteen minutes. A few people would get out, pushing and jerking and easing and gasping, then a few more would get in and we were off again. I asked my friend if he knew of any Christians along the coast. He told me there was a Christian in Shizunai. My interest was aroused and I asked him the name. 'Ega-san,' he said. 'He is really an old Ainu chief. He earns his money now by writing business and legal letters for many of the Ainu along the coast, not that there are many pure Ainu left here now. Most of them are inter-marrying.' As I looked around I could see what he meant. Many of the passengers were more swarthy than the normal Japanese and their lips were thicker. Some of them had wide eyes as well. Yes, I could see the strains of Ainu blood here and there. It is said that the Japanese did to the Ainu what they claim the Americans did to the Red Indians, they sold them liquor and then took their land away from them by getting them to sign papers when they were drunk. As a young man Ega hated the Japanese because of this. Then he came under the influence of Mr Batchelor, an Anglican clergyman who pioneered in that area, reducing the Ainu language to writing and translating the New Testament for them. Ega learned from Mr Batchelor that you must love your enemies. The Japanese were his enemies and he hated them. He told God all about this trouble and God gave him a new heart.

Before World War II Ega had been an evangelist together with a group of other men and had travelled widely through the country preaching the Gospel. But he felt that during the war he had compromised his position by not making a clear stand on idolatry. Everybody in Japan had been required to bow before the portrait of the Emperor but many Christians had avoided doing this. Ega said, 'I never actually bowed to the portrait, but I was so

small that I looked as if I was bowing anyway.
Many of my friends went to prison, but I avoided
trouble in this way. Now I feel guilty about it.' Still,
the man in the train was very impressed with Ega-
san, his clean living and his witness to Jesus Christ,
and I felt that this was encouraging indeed.

The atmosphere was getting a little thick. We
were weary and our heads ached. We had stopped
at innumerable small stations during the last two
hours. At last we jerked to a standstill at our station. 'Shizunai! Shizunai!' bawled over the loud-
speakers was music in our ears. The tradesfolk
with their huge packs got out first, and at last we
reached the door. A breath of cold air shocked us
into life again.

We looked around the platform. Many hurrying
figures sped on their homeward journey, but there
was no one to greet us. Strange. We had sent a telegram to Miss Pine, the house help, so surely she
would be there. Were we dreaming? We watched
the dark brown begrimed little train pull out of the
station and wondered what had happened. Although my 'bolshie' spirit has never really taken
kindly to the thought of employing maids, I got
round it by calling her our house help. The fact
of the matter was that both Olga and I were still
giving hours to language study, and both trying to
carry a full programme; also we needed somebody
who would interpret us to the local population, so I
guess the house help was necessary.

The work in Shizunai had been begun about a
year or so before when three lady missionaries had

moved into the town, but for various reasons they had moved on. Olga had actually been living with the last of these girls and had come up from Shizunai to Sapporo to get married, so she knew the way. Being just before Christmas it was cold, and there were flurries of snow. We decided to walk it. Just out of the railway station a couple of minutes, and then a left turn up an unmade road, almost an alley, with wooden shacks on both sides and uneven ground, and so we came to our house. Although it was fairly new, it was more of a shack than a house. The walls were unpainted boards and the roof thin metal sheeting painted green. We got into the porch and there was Miss Pine, looking very embarrassed indeed. What had gone wrong? She explained to us that the telegram had said 'Arriving by the four o'clock train'. She had looked in the railway timetable for a train at such a time, but there wasn't one, so she couldn't understand. Olga and I stood there and looked at each other. According to the railway timetable our train should arrive at 3.59. Why had this girl not been able to make the adjustment of one minute? Did she not want to be seen with the foreigners? Up until now she had only worked for the three lady missionaries. Now there was a man involved, was she taking umbrage at this? You don't have to live long in Japan before you begin to look for all kinds of hidden meanings.

Miss Pine was very much a peasant girl. Almost all Japanese women are graceful and easy in their movements, but she wasn't. She also had an unfortunate facial contortion and had been unable to find a husband, and she was without her parents. She knew that not meeting us at the train was just about an unforgivable sin by her society's patterns. Two things you must do in Japan are to see guests off to the railway station and make sure they get on the train, and to meet new guests arriving at the railway station, presumably to make sure they get off it. This she hadn't done. It wasn't a good start.

We stepped into the room. In Japan flooring is usually made up of two-inch-thick matting called *tatami*, six feet by three feet in size. You have a six-mat, and eight-mat or a ten-mat room, but you never have a four mat room because the word for four in Japanese is the same as the word for death, and this is a word to be avoided. So you have a four-and-a-half mat room — actually five-mat with half a mat cut away. This open space is filled with a fine sand and charcoal is burned in it. A frame of wood is placed over the hole and then over the frame is a heavy wadded blanket. In winter people sit with their feet in the hole, and wear thick wadded kimonos and thus keep warm. That is down south — that's not the way you keep warm in Hokkaido, at least not adequately.

The room we stepped into was eight-mat in size but the floor was made of a kind of plywood which swayed and curved as I walked across it. The walls were plain plywood too. There was a heavy kitchen cupboard at one side, and a wood-burning stove on a metal stand with a chimney that went straight up and then off at right angles through a window. Round two thirds of the room there were windows, thus making it what we called the 'goldfish bowl'. There were two other rooms at the back with big cupboards, where the bedding was kept. There were no beds in the room, but a heavy mattress was pulled out at night and a lighter quilt-like thing put over it, two sheets in between and that was our bed. We had two desks and two chairs, and when guests came we pulled out *zabuton* (small flat square cushions) and we all sat down on the floor round the low table.

So this was our first home. We seemed to have got off on the wrong foot with the house help, and the atmosphere was quite cool. Although we had been engaged for four years, our courtship had been a scrappy affair, with moments of guarded intensity followed by long periods of separation. It took me a long time to settle down to prayers together with Olga. I have discovered that this is so with other young married Christians, and I am sure that Satan attacks at this point too. As we get to know each other and each other's foibles and frailties, there is a danger of unreality in our prayers.

We unpacked a few things and sat down at the table as Miss Pine brought in our meal. This seemed somewhat unreal too. It was a bowl of rice with chicken fried together with eggs. It is called *oyako* which means literally 'mother and child' — the mother being the chicken, and the child being the egg. It had not been well cooked and there was a general sense of depression. That night the storm clouds came up and there was a howling gale with snow outside. Try as we would we couldn't get warm, no matter how many blankets we put on. The electric light failed, and the curtains seemed to be blowing at right angles from the window frames. We counted the hours during that miserable cold night, and in the morning we discovered that the wainscotting round the top of the walls hid a gap of about six inches right the way round. No wonder we hadn't been warm!

The earnest efforts of the lady missionaries who had occupied the house before us had resulted in people coming along. The trouble was that these missionaries were quite musical. It was great for them to get three or four young Japanese women around the harmonium and teach them to sing hymns in harmony. Olga could play the violin and I could play the mouth organ, but neither of us was particularly musical. On top of that the three young teachers who had become friends of these lady missionaries were used to their genteel ways, but weren't too much at home with me lumbering about the place.

We had our first Sunday morning service just the Sunday before Christmas. I spent the two days before it trying to prepare a Christmas message, which meant writing out a fair bit of it in English, then translating into Japanese, then reading it out to a Japanese person and asking him to correct it. It was some weeks before we discovered that a Japanese would never dream of correcting the foreigner, and so my mistakes remained hidden for a long time. That first Sunday morning, four people came into our house for the morning service. From about eight o'clock I had been busy with my English Bible and my Japanese Bible, writing out some kind of service, choosing hymns from the Japanese hymn book. Almost all of these hymns have come from the west, either from Europe or from England.

First Mr Ega arrived. I was thrilled to bits to discover just as soon as I got to Shizunai that not only was Mr Ega there, but he had thrown in his lot with us, and was coming along to our meeting. His background was in a Holiness group, who were given to outward expression of their inward experience. This meant that whenever I mentioned anything he agreed with, I got a 'Hallelujah' or 'Praise the Lord'. This warmed my own heart and helped me to get on with my sermon in Japanese. However, it really stumbled other preachers, making them forget their Japanese and lose the place in their notes.

After Ega came three ladies from the local school, who had been reached by our friends previously. I think one sight of me was enough because two of them never came back again, but the other teacher felt sorry for us in our apparent loneliness and often came in to visit us. In our back room there was a kind of alcove known as the *tokonoma*. Here a hanging scroll is usually put, and also some flower arrangement. One evening this young teacher arrived with some flowers and twigs to attempt a flower arrangement. She became quite enthusiastic as she cut off pieces here and pieces there, until finally there was nothing left. We could see that something had gone wrong somewhere although we didn't know what, and it was obvious to her that we knew. What an embarrassment! We weren't making too much progress in our first few weeks in Shizunai.

This town of fifteen thousand people was a real burden on my heart, for I saw myself as standing between the living and the dead. To me the risen Christ was the ruler of the universe, and when He said, 'I am the light of the world; I am the resurrection and the life; I am the bread of life', this was not egoism but actual fact. I believed that we had been called as missionaries to preach the Gospel of eternal life to those who were in darkness, to those who were without hope; and as far as I was concerned the vast majority of the citizens in Shizunai were outside Christ and without hope. My problem was how to make this known. Olga and I talked and prayed over the situation. It was winter time, getting on into the New Year. We thought we would have a week of meetings. We could get some bills printed announcing them, and we would preach on the seven 'I AMs'. I would preach and Olga would provide the music with her violin. We didn't try to cover the whole town at this stage, just the two or three hundred houses in our vicinity. The drill was to take some tracts and invitations, go along to the houses and walk into the porch. Japanese doors slide open with a grating sound, which lets people know you are there, and you then call out, '*Gomen kudasai*' which means 'please excuse me'. When they came to the door we said, 'Please read this and come along to our meetings'. Every person, I think without exception, said, 'Thank you very much, and almost certainly we will come.'

We got wildly excited about it all, and then the day before the meetings were to begin I went down with either heavy flu or bronchitis, and was out for the count. This left Olga who had to take over where I left off. We were praying and looking to the Lord for a real crowd to come to the house. In fact we didn't know what on earth we would do if all those who had said they would come did come. The meeting was due to begin at seven pm, and as it got nearer and nearer the time we put the chairs out and set up the little pulpit; Olga tuned her violin; we put out hymn sheets and then we waited. Ten past seven, twenty past seven, nobody came in. At half past seven the lady who had made our flower arrangements arrived and sat down. We greeted her and she bowed in return. At quarter to eight we decided we should have our meeting and so we began to teach her the first of the seven 'I AMs' of John. That is what we did for the remainder of that week.

Olga also inherited a girls' Bible class from the former missionaries. These girls were from the local high school. They always looked very solemn indeed and chose the saddest songs from the hymn book. Six or seven would come in in dark blue shirts and jackets, dark eyes and dark hair merging into the general gloom of our front room. From the other side of the glass partition, I would listen as my fellow worker attempted to awaken some spark of spiritual life in these girls.

Shizunai means literally 'inside the quiet'. I never

saw a town with such a misnomer in all my life. It was anything but quiet. There were two cinemas in the street and as you walked down the road you could hear the soundtrack from both of them — Humphrey Bogart/Lauren Bacall in one ear and a good cowboy movie soundtrack in the other. To add to this confusion, on every lamppost in the town there was a loudspeaker outfit, through which came announcements and music from seven in the morning till nine at night. Every local shop advertised through the tannoy system. At one time, when the high school students were studying for their end of term exams, it was so noisy that they put in a complaint to the mayor. After thinking about the problem he said he couldn't do anything since it would be interfering with people's livelihood.

Shizunai was a logging camp. The logs were brought down from the mountains, either floated or brought down on trucks, and in Shizunai they were sawn up and made into plywood, which went out all over the world. Every so often the logging men came down from the hills and, together with the men from the cutting factories, lit up the town. It was not a big place, but two or three streets had nothing but bars.

I walked round the town several times in the first few weeks that we lived there. Some of the people were friendly and would give a grin; others were shy and embarrassed and turned away. Some were hostile — you could see it in the fierceness of their eyes. Small children would draw back and call us *gaijin* (foreigners), 'come and see the *gaijin*'. That is just what we were — foreigners in this town. We had no place in their society or in their customs, and we hardly understood their language.

One day Katoo-san turned up at the meeting. (Everybody in Japan is 'san'. Mr, Mrs and Miss all gather under the term *san*.) Katoo-san had eight children and was as poor as a church mouse. He was also deformed. He had heard the Gospel over the radio and had trusted in Christ, and although he belonged to a church in another town, he came along to us for fellowship. As I got to know Ega better, he and I would go along to Katoo's tiny little house where the eight children all gathered round. There we would sing old hymns about fighting for the Lord and waiting for the fire of the Holy Spirit and the precious blood of Christ. We usually began together but we all finished in different places. Ega's approach to music was to get to the end of the verse just as quickly as he could. Katoo-san couldn't hear much of what was going on anyway so he sang in a silent world of his own and quite slowly. I took a middle course and finished up somewhere between the other two. After this we would pray together. We were not a very youthful-looking group to tackle the world, the flesh and the devil in the town of Shizunai.

As we got into January we were thinking and praying about some new outreach, and thought we should start a Bible class. We discovered that we could get advertising bills printed, ask the newsagent to interleave them in the local newspaper, and in this way cover the whole town. We had funds from the Mission to cover this kind of expense. Every missionary has his accounts, and the money came through every quarter as the Lord supplied. We had money for food, based on the local cost of living, money for rent, money for travel from one town to another when we were engaged in visitation or preaching, money for tracts and literature, and money that was loosely called 'evangelism'. All these accounts had to be sorted out and made to balance, and once a quarter we sent them in to the Superintendent's office. So we worked on the advertising leaflets, taking quite a time working out the best kind of Japanese sentences and making sure we didn't make any big mistakes. Two or three days before we wanted to start, we put these bills out through the local newspapers, as well as handing them out to people. In view of our disastrous week of campaign we were not too hopeful; so we were all the more surprised when the first Tuesday evening eight men came in, seven of them well-built solid pioneer men. I longed to see them brought to Christ.

I began with Romans 1. Even as I started in my poor Japanese, I was aware that every one of those phrases in the opening verses was loaded and needed hours of explanation. These people knew nothing of the true and living God. The Old Testament was nothing to them. All the promises of God to the people of Israel down through the years and the outworkings of the promises in Christ — they knew nothing of them. The relationship between David and Jesus meant nothing to them. Unless the Holy Spirit took the things of Christ and showed them to these men, I hadn't got a hope. Amongst them was one who had come in a bit late. He was different from the others, much shorter and smaller. His hair was shaved, and he was wearing an old pink tee-shirt and a dirty pair of trousers. As he came into the room, he kicked off a pair of dirty gym shoes before sitting down on the bench. His eyes were puffy and his face expressionless. I took one look at him and decided that he would never learn anything. He looked a moron.

After the Bible study we served Japanese tea in handleless cups together with biscuits, and we tried to talk a bit. They had questions, but we could only understand half the meaning. We longed for some Japanese fellow worker who would be able to interpret for us and help us. We were the only Mission who had ever attempted to work in Japan without fellow workers, and Olga and I were really feeling it right then. The tramp-like young fellow had refused tea and biscuits and left quite early. When everybody had gone, the two of us had a praise meeting, thanking God for bringing in that handful of people. We asked God to work in their hearts, and in their minds, and that somehow we might make Him known to them. We didn't think of including the scruffy-looking chap, or at least I didn't. I said to Olga, 'He won't be back any more'. She replied, 'Well, let's have more faith than that'. That evening our hearts were light and we saw that God could work.

The next morning, although the snow was on the ground, we could see the sun hitting the roof of the barn across the way. Around nine o'clock our front door opened with a rattle. I opened the inner glass door and looked at the drop-out that we had seen the night before. He said something about wanting to talk and that he had some questions and could he come in. I let him in and got my Bible, and away he went talking nineteen to the dozen. I hadn't a clue what he was talking about, but I did catch one word which I thought was *bokushi*, the Japanese word for pastor. And also he was mentioning Tokyo and Shizuoka, so that I thought that this man, Nakagawa-san, had met up with a pastor in Tokyo or Shizuoka. What was I to do? I just lifted up my heart in prayer to the Lord and said, 'Show me what to show him'. Then I said, 'You read this,' and turned over the pages of the Japanese Bible to Luke 15, and got him to read the story of the Prodigal Son. As he read it, he knew that this was just for him. He wasn't saying *bokushi;* he was saying *bokusa* (boxer).

At fifteen Nakagawa-san had run away from home here in Shizunai and gone down south, where he had gone into a boxing club and pretty soon was on the way to being a champion. Then he got into a gang. There is a whole hierarchy of the gang system in Japan, and he was a member of one of the minor organizations peddling forbidden things, associated with protection rackets and so on. He was living in a dirty old lodging house at the time and the *mama-san* of the house wanted to be rid of him. 'Get out of here,' she said, 'you are more trouble than you are worth.' Nakagawa had no idea why this was, but he felt that the time had come for him to go home. He looked at the money he had and reckoned that he could just buy a ticket as far as Shizunai where his mother lived. He couldn't afford an express ticket and the slow train would take him three days. So he went to the ticket office and said, 'Shizunai — one please'. This took all his money and he just sat in the train as it crawled north, stopping at every station. When he was thirsty he got off and drank at one of the fountains on the platform. Food vendors went up and down the train, but Nakagawa had no money — all he could do was look at the food and turn away. So he reached Shizunai and went home.

He wasn't too happy about being seen by some of his old cronies in the town; he kept away from them. One day an old woman came to the house, visiting his mother. As they kneeled down on the *tatami* sipping their tea, the old woman suddenly turned to Nakagawa and said, 'What you need is religion'. Religion! He had never thought much about that, but it might be something he should try; then a man came and invited him to a Seventh Day Adventist meeting. He went along and got a full dose of the Ten Commandments. As he went back to his house he scratched his head and thought, 'Well, it's no good me joining that outfit, because I've broken all their rules before I start it.' Now here he was reading this story of a young boy who had gone away and wasted everything and then come back home. How did this foreign missionary know all his background? What was it all about anyway?

I had no idea then, of course, what was going on in his mind. I had learned a few basic sentences for showing a person his need of Christ, and I trotted one of these out. I said to him, 'Nakagawa, do you know what you are? You are a sinner. You have broken God's law.' Nakagawa looked at me, his face expressionless. Then I said to him, 'But Christ died for your sins'. He must have stayed about two hours. Just how much he took in, I don't know, and I don't think he did afterwards either. He was back every day for two, three or four hours. These times with him completely wore me out as I struggled to find sufficient Japanese. There was a real change in him too in those months, and the people in the area knew something had happened to him. Previously children had run away from him when they passed him in the street, but now he would get a few of them round him and talk to them about Jesus. We ran a Sunday School on Sunday mornings and Nakagawa asked us if he could come along to it. I said, 'Why, do you want to help?' 'No,' he said, 'I don't want to help. I want to sit in with the children and learn the things they are being taught. I'm a child in this and I need to know.'

When I had lived with David Hayman back in the Kutchan days, he was just that little bit better at Japanese than I was. So when we had visitors, and I had had enough, I would often leave David to it with the visitor. This meant, of course, that his Japanese became even better. Now I was having forced conversational training every day and, what was more, in things to do with the Christian faith, and I saw this as God's provision. The Lord knew what He wanted to train me for.

I was amazed at Nakagawa's growth in understanding. One day his Seventh Day Adventist friends came down and began to speak to him about the need to keep Saturday as the day of worship. I took no part in the conversation at all but left him to it. Suddenly he turned to them and said, 'Look, if you add anything to the cross of Christ, then I'm done. I've got no hope other than what Christ did on the cross for me.' His friends got up and went away.

Then there was the veterinary surgeon. Sometimes you meet people you just wish were in the kingdom of God, and I wished it for that man; his heart was open too. Tuesday evenings he would come into the porch, take off his shoes and come in and bow and sit down. One of the things which puzzled him was the term 'righteousness', being justified by faith, being made righteous by faith. The Japanese term is a very difficult one anyway, and I tried to get its meaning across to him. He had been coming for about three months when he turned up one evening in quite a state. He had a problem and wanted to know what a Christian should do. He was saying that in Japanese Buddhism, every morning the person in the house bowed down before the *butsudan* (family altar) and offered up rice and other things to the spirits of the dead relatives. I couldn't get his point at all, and we must have been together there for all of the evening. Although I prayed with him before he went, I realized I hadn't got through to him. Why was it that this man who was educated as a vet and therefore had college training couldn't understand the Word of God whereas drop-out Nakagawa had grasped it? From that evening the vet attended less and less at the Tuesday evening meetings, until suddenly he was moved further down the coast and we didn't see him any more.

Nakagawa had a problem too. Sometime in his conversation with me I had shown him the place in the Bible where it says, 'If you faint in the day of adversity, your strength is small. Rescue those who are being taken away to death. Hold back those who are stumbling to the slaughter. If you say, "Behold we did not know this," does not he who weighs the heart perceive it? Does not he who keeps watch over your soul know it and will he not requite man according to his work?' Nakagawa thought a lot about this verse. It seemed to him that there were many who were being taken away to death, who were stumbling on to slaughter. To him it all pointed to the day of judgement, and Nakagawa couldn't get away from his own responsibility. He took his Japanese Bible one evening and went up on the hills above Shizunai where he could look over the city and over the sea. He knelt down and prayed, spending hours wrestling with this problem. Why was God speaking to him about the needs of others? He had no education, no qualifications, no standing in the town. Everybody knew what he had been. He wrestled a long time, and finally he surrendered. He said, 'God if you want me to do this, if you want me to rescue those who are being taken away to death, and to hold back those who are stumbling to the slaughter, then you will have to give me the power, and you will have to help me to understand Your Word.' It was then that. God began to show Nakagawa not power, but the meanness of his own heart. As the moments passed, he saw almost in a mirror, his own meanness and wildness and darkness. As the sun came up out of the sea, a great red ball of flame, so the Holy Spirit came in and took possession of Nakagawa. All night he had been there, and God met with him.

Another man I knew had a similar experience. He was a minister in the United Church of Japan, who had had a very simple faith; but when he went to theological seminary the new teaching puzzled him and he found he was drifting and was uncertain about everything. He took his New Testament and Luther's Commentary on Galatians and went up into a little hut in the mountains, where he fasted and prayed for four days. He told me that when he came out of that hut, he had assurance of salvation, and has never wavered from it since.

Nakagawa had been coming to us almost daily for three months, and I had still not talked to him about his personal belief. One day he arrived bustling and cheerful as usual, a very different man from the morose person who had first come to our house. He kicked his shoes off, toe against heel, pushed open the door and stepped inside. We pushed out the *zabutons*, sat down and opened our Bibles.

'Nakagawa,' I said, 'you need to have a real trust in Jesus Christ. You need to ask Him to save you.'

Limitation of language kept me from being too technical. He looked at me in surprise.

'You don't need to worry about me, Abruhamususan, God has filled me with His Spirit. First He showed me my sin, then He showed me Jesus. Now I am born again.'

I looked at him, absolutely amazed at this work of God.

Then he said, 'I want to be baptized.'

I took a deep breath. This would be my first baptism in Japan, and I felt that I mustn't make any mistakes.

'You ought to have some more teaching first.'

'Why? Where does it say that in the Bible?' He had me there, but I had another problem and that was where to baptize him. With the snows beginning to melt in the mountains, the river was cold and in flood.

'I want to be baptized now.' So we decided on it.

There were a few people coming along to the Sunday morning meetings by now: Ega-san the Ainu of course, two or three high school girls, a game warden from up in the hills and some others, making about ten in number. But apart from Ega, Nakagawa was really the only one with faith. We decided to have a baptismal service at the riverside on Sunday morning in place of our usual service. We were a bit scared, wondering how it was all going to work out; here was a handful of half-believers who had never seen such a thing before.

The water was black and murky, flowing fast. The wind was up too. We sang some hymns and the wind snatched our voices away. We bowed in prayer. The onlookers stood huddled on the bank, feeling the cold. I walked slowly into the river bracing myself against the stream, and after the initial plunge, felt tremendously exhilarated. God was good. He had given us our first fruit. Nakagawa was much smaller than me, and he walked in more carefully. Together we stood there.

'Do you not know that all of us who have been baptized into Christ Jesus were baptized into His death? We were buried therefore with Him by baptism into death so that as Christ was raised from the dead by the glory of the Father, we too might walk in newness of life.' Here it was, Nakagawa the outcast, the drop-out, made a new man in Jesus. Praise God!

'I baptize you Nakagawa Akira in the Name of the Father and of the Son and of the Holy Spirit.' It was glorious but it wasn't all that dignified. Having pushed him under, I nearly lost him, but after a struggle, we both stood upright and walked out. Here were the beginnings in Shizunai.

10
OUTREACH

THE JAPAN EVANGELISTIC Band had used tents to advantage in the south of Japan before the war, and since then lots of other missionaries had followed their example. Dave Hayman in Kutchan and I in Shizunai wanted to have a go at it too, so we applied to the Superintendent for funds for the tent. It was made a special matter for prayer, and as the money became available we were able to buy a gleaming white tent for evangelism along the Hidaka coast. (Some years later we had a fantastic answer to prayer when we needed to get a tent renewed. I wrote to our Superintendent, who by then was Dave Hayman himself, asking him for money for a tent for evangelism in north Japan. He opened my letter and read it, and then went through other letters on his desk. One was from our headquarters in Singapore, in which was a credit slip stating that US$400 for a tent for evangelism in northern Japan had been donated by a businessman in Guatemala! We wrote to thank him and sent him photographs of the tent but we never heard from him personally.)

I asked David Hayman to come down to the Hidaka to help us, and we planned evangelistic meetings in about four places. Two missionary ladies were working in the town of Mombetsu, an hour away from us one way, and Don and Winnie Morris from Canada were an hour and a half or so away in the other direction. So we thought we would include these two towns and maybe one or two others. Dave reckoned he could preach for fifteen or twenty minutes without notes, and I thought I could do the same. We planned to use slides of the life of Christ, and reckoned that Nakagawa (who hadn't got a job yet and so was free to help) would give a testimony, and maybe there would be other Christians who could also tell of their personal experience of Christ. We wanted to make sure that everybody in these towns would have an opportunity to hear of the Saviour, our Lord Jesus Christ.

Nakagawa and I went to Mombetsu and talked to Lucille Hall and her fellow-worker. We walked round the small shanty town and found an open space between two buildings which would do for the tent. The owners gave permission, and we had bills and posters printed, inviting people to hear 'what the Bible says about God, about Jesus Christ and about you'. We walked round the town pinning up posters on every corner, and visited every home with leaflets.

Putting up the tent was an advertisement in itself. A group of small children with dark hair and dark eyes, the little girls in brightly-coloured *kimono*, stood around watching. A woman with a child on her back and shopping basket in her hand stopped for a bit. Others passed along. The word was getting around.

We had heard from a lady in Tokyo who knew

someone she thought could be of tremendous help to us. He was Chinese, very fluent in Japanese, a very spiritual man whom God was using mightily. He sounded a little like an Asian Billy Graham. We were pleased when we heard that this Mr Lee was coming up to help us, and we met him at the station. He was quite fat and wobbled a bit as he walked. Dave Hayman, Nakagawa and I were sleeping in the tent, but in view of Mr Lee's position we had put him in the local Japanese inn.

An old Japanese inn has long dark cool corridors with small rooms leading off from the corridor on either side. The heavy cardboard doors slide back on runners. At the door you take off your shoes and put on slippers, and at your room you take off your slippers and step on to the *tatami* matting. The furniture consists of a low table in the centre of the room and two or three small mats for sitting on; in one corner is an alcove which usually contains a hanging picture with a proverb on it, and underneath it a bowl of flowers with a Japanese motif. (The Japanese do a lot with a little, and our way of pushing a lot of flowers into a vase would leave them horrified.) Soon after you arrive at the inn, the Japanese maid comes along and invites you to take your bath. There is a low wooden tray in the room on which you put your clothes, and pick up the thin *kimono* with its long waist-band. The maid then leads you along to the bathroom, and on your return she brings in your meal which is usually rice with fish, soup and vegetable, almost always cold.

We showed Mr Lee to his room and invited him

to come along to the tent the following morning. We had the tent up by then; we learned its mysteries and unfolded it and put up the big poles and hammered in the tent pegs, and there it was. Next day we took leaflets to every home in Mombetsu and preached on every street corner, and all this time Mr Lee sat in the tent. David felt he should have a word with him, so he went up to him and said, 'Pardon us for leaving you sitting in this tent all the time while we go out and tell the people about Jesus Christ.' He smiled as he thumbed through his New Testament. 'I don't mind sitting here quietly as long as I have my New Testament and I can meet with the Lord.' It was at this stage that we discovered he only preached if the Lord was moving him. I have met other people like this since. For me it is a simple matter: there is a general command to preach the Gospel to every creature and to be at work in season and out of season; I think that about covers everything. I do know in my preaching that sometimes I feel I have a message from God and at other times I am battling a bit; but it seems to me that if you seek the Lord and obey His command, then He will do what He wants to do.

That evening after the tent meeting I took Mr Lee back to his hotel room. We squatted on the small mats and he said earnestly to me, 'You know, people should be praying for this tent evangelism'. I replied, 'We have people all over the world praying for these meetings'. That seemed to cheer him up a bit.

We began again about four o'clock the following

afternoon, rounding up all the children. They came into the tent laughing and talking, and settled down on the rush mats we had put out on the earth. We taught them a song and told a story. Then they went home and we began again with the adults. They came in much more slowly and in a much more dignified manner. A few men sat at the back, and we could get no one to come forward until the tent began to fill up a bit. Mr Lee decided to preach, so with Dave giving his fifteen minutes and me giving my fifteen minutes and Mr Lee adding a bit they really heard quite a lot.

Among the people who came in that night was a young man who had been in the beer trade in Manchuria. When the Russians went in right at the end of the war, Mr Okuda was picked up along with thousands of others. However, as he knew something about brewing beer they kept him there for a couple of years. He learned about Communism and Marxism and they learned how to brew beer Japanese fashion. When he was released and came back to Japan, the Government gave him a piece of land out north of Mombetsu, and he got on with trying to develop it. He also began to buy fish from the fishermen at the wharf-side and sell it round the town, pushing it around in boxes on an old barrow. He came along to the tent out of interest, listened to us all and decided that the person who had the most Japanese and would be able to understand him was Mr Lee. As the people dwindled out of the tent and some stood around looking at the posters on the tent walls, Mr Lee and Mr Okuda sat down on the floor of the tent and Mr Okuda spent a good fifteen minutes proving the non-existence of God. At the end of this Mr Lee bowed his head and prayed, 'Oh God, this young man is filled with the sense of his own importance. He is so blind that I cannot do anything to help him. Perhaps you can. Amen.' Then he opened his eyes, got up and walked away. It was certainly a new approach to personal work. Mr Okuda went home in high dudgeon. He couldn't see how it was that he had proved satisfactorily to himself that God didn't exist, and then Mr Lee quite blatantly prayed to the God who presumably wasn't there.

It troubled Mr Okuda all day, and he felt he ought to go along to the tent the following evening. He sat through the efforts of the missionaries to teach the people the strange Christian songs, and then went on listening to the things they were saying. Something began to worry Mr Okuda. According to these people he was a sinner; and according to the way they explained it, he could see that he was. Supposing there was a God after all? There must be something after death. These fellows seemed to be very sure of themselves, and yet they weren't speaking arrogantly. He decided to have another talk with Mr Lee. After the meeting Mr Lee didn't seem to be there so he approached me.

'Can I see the big fat man?' he said. I looked round for Mr Lee and saw he was in the corner in earnest conversation with two grandmothers, kneeling on the floor in dark *kimono*, their grey hair drawn back tightly from the forehead. I went up to

Mr Lee and said, 'That man who was in last night, he would like to talk to you'. Mr Lee looked at me with a bland smile.

'I have nothing from God for him tonight,' he said, and turned back to the old ladies. I relayed the message to Mr Okuda and off he went.

As Mr Okuda sees it now, the Holy Spirit of God worked in his heart and mind throughout the following day, and by the evening he was almost in despair. He had to get to that tent and he had to get there as quickly as possible, and he had to see Mr Lee. He sat on the floor impatiently as we went through the preliminaries of the hymn singing and advertising the booklets and explaining the way of salvation, and finally it was all over. He rushed up to Mr Lee.

'You've got to help me,' he said, 'I must find God.' Very simply Mr Lee brought him into the presence of the Saviour.

All that week the tent was pretty well filled, and they listened well to all that we had to say; but apart from Mr Okuda there was very little apparent result. However, I had seen in action a man who seemed to be in direct contact with God in a greater detail than I knew.

So we moved on to Shizunai our home town, and again went through the programme of finding a vacant lot, putting up posters, giving out handbills, putting the tent up, pinning the posters round the walls, bringing in the little organ and the wooden pulpit and the hymn sheets and the amplifying equipment, getting permission for electricity from a local shop. The tent filled, the people leaning forward as they crouched on the straw matting. A little central aisle revealed hard earth down the middle of the tent. Up front was the screen for the slides, and hymn sheets hanging. As we sang a verse of 'Only believe' we explained its meaning, and as we taught them the song 'There is only one God' we explained Who He was, and what He could be to them. I think the tent was full every night.

The first day in Shizunai, I took Mr Lee along to a local eating house. It was fairly well packed with people getting their bowl of noodle lunch, and we ordered ours. We had been sitting there for a moment chatting when a young woman came up and stroked Mr Lee's knee. I had had this kind of experience once before, but had just explained that I was a Christian and given the lady a John's Gospel. Mr Lee was totally unprepared for this situation. He wobbled in aroused indignation and told her to go away. From that time on, he preached the Word powerfully and with feeling in Shizunai. God had told him to preach.

All that week, although the people came into the tent, although they sat there quietly and listened, there was no response. It was as though the words were like stones being thrown into a frozen pool. They did not penetrate, but skidded away to the side. One evening towards the end of the week Mr Ega, the bearded ageing Ainu, preached with real fervency on Noah and the flood. On the following morning, David Hayman left to go back to his station, and I went down to look at the tent. I noticed the ground was wet, so I got the equipment out and brought it back. When I went back to the tent again a little later it was under two feet of water and I had difficulty getting the sides of the tent free; and still the water from the flooding river came in until two-thirds of the town was under anything up to five feet of water. It was like this all along the coast. At Miikappu nineteen people died when the flood came in. When I heard about this, I remembered how Nakagawa and I had visited some young men in hospital there. Miikappu is about two miles from Shizunai, and every time a truck passed you on the earth coastal road you were covered from head to foot in dust. Now and again, sharp stones turned your ankle over. The sun was hot on your face and the breeze cool on your back. It was when we were walking back after visiting these men that Nakagawa said to me, 'Can't we just tell them that they have got to believe?' But you can't do it that way.

The net result of our meetings in Shizunai was minus rather than plus. It wasn't just that the people who had heard the Gospel didn't want to know, but even those who had been coming along now dropped off. We had a thriving little Sunday School which Olga had taught every week, but after the tent meetings none of the children came. We got the room ready, prepared the flannelgraph message, and Nakagawa went round with the loud-speaker, reminding children of the day and time, but nobody came. The adult meeting was the same: Faithful Ega was with us, and staunch Nakagawa, but up through the August of that year we were hitting rock bottom.

Nowadays, living in a town where there are several churches although they are small, I don't have the same sense of urgency that I had then. Maybe it's because I've cooled off. I felt that in Shizunai we stood between the living and the dead. But even so I felt the stuffing knocked out of me by this lack of response, and felt that in part at least the Mission was to blame. The people at our headquarters in Singapore seemed far away, and weren't able to appreciate all that was involved in being the only mission not working with Japanese help. Every other missionary was working with a Japanese pastor or evangelist. Time and again I had been questioned about things and had been unable to understand what was being said. The Lord could work in spite of our weaknesses, yet He didn't appear to be doing so.

One evening in August I picked up 'Daily Light' and idly flipped over the pages to the reading for the day, August 24. It said:

'I must work the works of him that sent me, while it is day. The soul of the sluggard desireth, and hath nothing; but the soul of the diligent shall be made fat. He that watereth shall be watered.

'My meat is to do the will of him that sent me, and to finish his work. Say not ye, There are yet four months, and then cometh harvest? behold, I say unto you, Lift up your eyes, and look on the fields; for they are white already to harvest. And he that reapeth receiveth wages, and gathereth fruit unto life eternal; that both he that soweth and he that reapeth may rejoice together. — The kingdom of heaven is like unto a man that is an householder, which went out early in the morning to hire labourers into his vineyard. And when he had agreed with the labourers for a penny a day, he sent them into his vineyard. — Preach the word; be instant in season, out of season. — Occupy till I come.'

These verses hit me, and came as a direct challenge to go out into the street and preach again. I walked alone down the main street, feeling the strangeness of a foreign culture, the half-understood language, the glances of the people and the noise. As usual, every shop was blaring out its advertisements and music. The soundtracks of the two films showing, the proclamations from every loudspeaker on the telegraph poles, and me in the middle. I didn't know what I could do in all the racket! The words which I had read a few minutes previously and which had burned into my mind and heart so much were now receding, and I felt a bit of a fool. I half turned towards one or two groups of young men hanging about on the corners. Their cold stares and half-turned shoulders put me off. I spoke almost audibly: 'Lord, if you will stop all this noise then I will preach.'

This half prayer of despair was hardly sent heavenward when suddenly the whole town was bathed in quietness. The miracle can be easily explained: it was a power cut, not an unusual thing in Shizunai in those days. The fact that it came in answer to prayer is not so easily rationalized. I stood there on the street corner and began to put up a poster saying 'The wages of sin is death but the free gift of God is eternal life'. Two young women from the local bar came out and helped me pin it up. I wished that there had been other kind of help too, but I stood there alone and preached Christ, trying to give out tracts at the same time. Almost in a dream, I saw them coming round, young men and old men, high school boys and girls. A teacher at the high school who had been to our meeting in the past hurried along, stopping just for a moment. A Buddhist priest from the temple came and bowed in front of me, saying *'Gokuroosama'* ('I appreciate what you are doing'). Some Buddhist sects are quite hostile to Christianity, whereas others regard Christianity as part of the world's religion anyway, and are quite affable. So as the sun went down and the shadows along the road grew longer, I stood there preaching while they listened. When I could hold their attention no more, and my insufficient language took its toll, I came back home.

11
NIGHT AND MORNING

IN JAPAN MANY MEN go to the medical schools of the larger universities and then do a year or two in internship. After they graduate, somebody in the family puts up some money and they begin a local hospital. This is really something between the old general practitioner in England and a small clinic. It may or may not have two or three small wards for in-patients. The nurses do not touch the catering side, at least they used not to, but a relative moves in with the patient to look after him or her.

Roslyn Hayman is a doctor, and a very good one at that, but she had come to Japan as a missionary evangelist and Bible teacher rather than to practise medicine. The OMF didn't have any medical work in Japan, but Roslyn had been asked to look after a clinic for a mission somewhere down south. So it was decided that when our baby was nearly due, Olga would travel down there, stay with Roslyn and have the baby there. It didn't occur to me that I should be with Olga at that time, and we had decided that I would stay in Shizunai while she was in Kitakami in the south, and then go down and collect her when the baby was born.

We had one final set of tent meetings further along the coast where Canadian workers Don and

Winnie Morris were living, and a couple of older missionaries who had been in China came along to help too. We were in the train travelling back to Shizunai when old China hand Mrs Hazelton asked me if I was going to be with Olga during her confinement. I cracked on real hardy and said I hadn't been thinking of doing so; I didn't know that that was the thing that missionaries do. She told me, 'It's a good thing for a husband to be with his wife when the child is born, especially if it happens to be the first one. I think you ought to go down.' When I got back to Shizunai I got in touch with the Superintendent, and I realized again how easily communications can get mixed up. He said that I certainly ought to be with my wife, but as I hadn't approached him he had assumed that it was some personal arrangement between the two of us and hadn't liked to interfere.

The building I stayed in near the clinic was an old Japanese farmhouse with large rooms, high ceilings and dark smoky beams. There was an Akita hound, rather like an Alsatian, which was kept chained outside and howled at intervals. During the day I would do some language study and Bible study, and then go down to see how Olga was getting along. One day Roslyn called me over and asked me to sit down. 'I need to talk to you,' she said.

Do you ever get the feeling that bad news is coming before you hear it? I did that day.

Roslyn began, 'I have bad news for you: I can't hear the child's heart-beat. It was there two days ago but I can't hear it now. Olga herself is well, there is no obvious cause. I have been waiting, hoping for better things, but I need to tell you now. You will have to tell Olga.' As Roslyn went on talking to me I could feel the room going round. We had waited so long for marriage and for this first child. I was glad I was sitting down, and tried to pull myself together.

Olga seemed so full of hope and so defenceless, and I had to say that it was no-go. So I told her, 'The child is dead'. And she wept, and so did I. It was the longest night of our lives. Roslyn had said there was no reason why Olga should not have other children, but I had not understood this, and had it firmly fixed in my mind that there now was a real possibility of not having a family.

As the baby was due in a few days' time it was decided to induce labour. Roslyn had wished she had better blood transfusion equipment, although two members of the staff were ready with compatible blood should it be needed. This wish became more acute when it turned out that Olga had placenta praevia, which could easily have required large transfusions. But in the goodness of the Lord no blood was needed at all, and Olga had a normal blood count after the baby was born.

Returning alone from the clinic to the old farmhouse, I was full of resentment and anger against God. Why should it happen to her? I felt that I had been such a sinner anyway, anything God did to me I deserved; but I just couldn't understand why it had happened to my wife. I felt that God was getting back at me through her. These were some of the crazy thoughts that were running through my head. I turned to the regular reading of my Bible more as a habit than because I wanted to, and I opened it at Isaiah chapter 49 and read verse 20: 'The children which thou shalt have after thou hast lost the other shall say again in thine ears, the place is too straight for me. Give place to me that I may dwell.' I could hardly believe the evidence of my own eyes — here was God's Word straight to me. I had a real fear that we would not have any children, and there were other problems too, yet here was God saying directly to me in spite of all my resentment, 'the children which you shall have'. I couldn't praise the Lord yet, but here was a promise.

After the delivery and the disposal of the little girl's body, I went into Olga's room. Immediately I sensed the presence of Christ. Olga was sitting up in bed with her head against the pillows, and she was radiant. The Lord had shown Himself to her, and in the midst of her suffering and disappointment she was full of the joy of the Lord. I felt that the ground on which I was walking was holy, and we were able to pray together.

And so we came back to our house in Shizunai, just the two of us. We had left with high hopes and we returned with nothing. Miss Matsuura, the girl who gave us help most mornings, was there to greet us. I couldn't analyse her attitude. Part of it, I think, was real sympathy, but there was a part which said, 'Your religion doesn't seem to have done much for you'. Many Japanese people like the kind of religion that gives you good luck, but anything that brings you bad luck is, of course, not worth having.

Matsuura-san seemed to have had some faith when we first arrived in Shizunai, and at that time was reading her Bible and showing signs that she was a Christian. Then one day she told us, 'My father asked me to take flowers to the *butsudan*'. The *butsudan*, a small shrine which is in most Japanese homes, enshrines the spirits of a dead parent or parents. The Japanese feel that the dead are wandering spirits, and that they have a responsibility to placate or to encourage those spirits. Failure to do this is lack of filial piety. Maybe it's not too much to say that you can be as unfeeling as you like towards your parents during their lives, but it would be an extremely evil person who did not carry out the simple rites before the *butsudan* every morning. These consist of putting a little bowl of rice and a cup of *ocha* (Japanese tea) or some other drink in the *butsudan*, clapping one's hands and offering up a prayer to the spirits.

Matsuura-san's father had come to her in a dream and said, 'I am lonely. Can't you offer up flowers?' In other words, 'bring some flowers along to the *butsudan* and just place them there and offer up a little prayer.' I suppose for many people this may seem an unimportant thing. When you think of all the terrific ethical and moral teaching contained in the Bible, why worry about offering up a few flowers to a spirit who probably isn't there anyway? What I personally believe is that this very simple act of worship is idolatry. It binds the Japanese people. Maybe we still need the Japanese theologian who will show from the Scriptures that we can have a proper filial piety and yet not engage in spirit worship.

Matsuura-san had taken the flowers, in spite of our warning, and put them on the *butsudan*. From that day her faith was gone. She lacked any desire to study the Bible. She wanted no prayer with us and she was a stranger.

At home in England, when a couple lost a child there would be friends and relatives calling to offer encouragement. There would be the warmth of some evangelical fellowship on Sunday. Here in this little town on the sea coast of Hokkaido there was neither. We were hitting rock bottom, and it was autumn.

The Japanese are very sensitive to nature. Because of their lack of belief in a creator God and their basic pantheism, they see themselves as part of nature. One Japanese challenged me on the verse in Genesis about subduing the earth — he claimed it was the Christian faith that had caused pollution! To him nature was not there to subdue, but rather to identify with. Earthquakes, volcanoes, typhoons, the rugged cliffs of the coastline, the crashing sea, the quietness of autumn, the bright full moon; all these enter into the very spirit of the Japanese. Autumn is the time of death, when leaves fall from the trees and flowers wither. The rice fields, just a few weeks previously golden with the abundance of harvest, are now barren. Autumn is a good time for evangelism in Japan, because people begin to think about the shortness of life and about the possibility of death. There is an indefinable sadness in the

Japanese mood in autumn, and we had come back to Shizunai at the time when the leaves fall from the trees.

After a day or two, dear old Ega appeared on the doorstep, pushing back the glass door, bowing low to us and responding to our welcome. Nakagawa came too, and we sensed his unvoiced sympathy. Even so, September and October were lonely months.

About that time two books came to my hand. One was called 'By My Spirit', three words from a text in Zechariah which reads, 'Not by might, nor by power, but by My Spirit says the Lord'. It's a word to a group of refugees returning to their former homeland, seeing around them devastation and decay. They have no power in government, nor miliary might, but God's Word to them is that by the very power of God through His Spirit they would see the land rejoice again, and the temple built. This book is about Jonathan Goforth, a Canadian Presbyterian missionary who went to China and then tö Korea. God used him in a startling way in revival. It is obvious from reading the book that it was only after years of obedience and dedication that he was used by God in this particular way. As he preached, God moved in on the community that he was speaking to; there was no half-hearted wondering if this was the truth or not, but rather a conviction which came so strongly upon the hearts and minds of the hearers that they were broken down.

This was something which I longed to see. Certainly we had no power and no might, no particular standing in the town, no big financial programme to put up a church building or an orphanage or to do something which would show the people that we were concerned about them.

The other book I read at that time was entitled 'The Revival we need' by Oswald Smith, pastor of the People's Church in Toronto, whose ministry God had certainly blessed. In a time when controversy was rife in America, Oswald Smith held firmly to the doctrine 'No defence, no attack'. By this he meant that he would not defend himself against the calumnies of others, neither would he attack personalities, although there was no doubt about his view of modernism and everything else which denied the significance of the death of Christ. In his book Oswald Smith showed clearly how weak and ineffectual the church so often was, and that this was not God's purpose.

These two books, both similar in that they pointed to the possibility of the sovereign work of God in revival, appealed to me. We knew the need for revival in our own hearts. We needed a touch from God to convince us of His power, and to convince the people around us.

I was particularly concerned at that time that we and others should see the glory of God. This was a new angle for us. We had thought in terms of the need for people to be saved, to know the love of Christ; but now we began to see that people were held in bondage and that this very bondage was dishonouring to their Maker. It wasn't God's purpose, nor to His glory, that they should believe in other things or worship other things. Just at this time we heard that there was a new Buddhist temple being built across the road. For some reason this really taunted Olga, and she just couldn't accept it. At the time when we appeared to be defeated, the enemy was triumphing over us by putting up yet another place which could not point the way to eternal life, nor show the way of victory over sin for it. So one night she simply asked the Lord to do something to show His glory. We can't prove that God did it, any more than we can prove He stopped the noise that time; but that temple was still unfinished several years later. Apparently the priest who was to be responsible for the temple had died, so the project came to be regarded as unlucky or even accursed.

I spent my days feeding on the Word and teaching Nakagawa-san. His early humility was beginning to pall, and he was feeling his wings. One day he came to me and said, 'Abruhamusu-san, I am going to be an evangelist just like you'. I believed that God was preparing him for something like this, but didn't think it was the right time yet. So I replied, 'You shouldn't think about evangelism. You should think about doing some good hard work. You haven't done any work all your life. People will believe that you are a Christian when they see you doing some work.' He obviously didn't like this very much, but I was surprised and pleased when I found he had a job working on the roads!

The burden of evangelism was still with me. I would walk out of our house, turn left up a bank, walk through a timber yard between piles of logs and come out on the beach. There I would walk up and down, oblivious of the wind and the waves, seeking the Lord's face and His power.

We must have been back in Shizunai about a month when there was a visitor to see us. It was Mr Kuga, the high school teacher who had passed the open air meeting I had had on the night when the noise stopped. Once or twice earlier he had come along to the meetings with us and we had visited his home. He was a Seventh Day Adventist and seemed to have a real faith. He was well known and liked in the school and he and his wife often had ten or a dozen boys and girls crowding into his small room to study the Bible. He came in and sat down. Olga made the inevitable Japanese tea, poured it out and pushed it toward him. He bowed in recognition, looking up at the ceiling and down to the floor. We wondered what his business was, but were content to wait and see. After one or two general remarks, he came to it. 'A few weeks ago you were in the street preaching, weren't you?' I nodded in assent, and he continued, 'As I passed your meeting I wanted to stop, but I was busy because I had to go to the school. That night God spoke to me and said. "This is the man you should work with", so now I've come.'

I looked at him in amazement. As simple as this! Here was our first answer to prayer. Mr Kuga and his wife started coming regularly and threw their weight in with us. They introduced us to many high school boys and girls, some of whom began coming along to Olga's Bible class. There were three girls who were especially keen. Mikado-san was tall for a Japanese and slim, with a very sweet face and expression. Sugimoto-san's father was the headmaster of a small elementary school in a town just along the line. She had quite a personality and was popular with everybody. Whereas Mikado-san was quiet and retiring, Sugimoto-san was much more at ease in company, even that of foreigners. The third girl was Kitajima-san. She was shorter than the other two and her features were square, her black hair straight down, her eyes always questioning. She was the philosopher of the three. She had read Nietsche and Goethe and other western philosophers; the problems of war and peace and of the purpose of living were always with Kitajima-san. These three girls began to help in the Sunday School, and together with Nakagawa to build it up. It wasn't long before that room at the front was once again filled, and this time even more than filled with children. They came piling into the room, kicking off their shoes in the *genkan*, taking their places round the wall and filling up the blank spaces.

Encouraged by all this, we began the Tuesday night Bible study class again, and through this we had other contacts. One of my big discouragements in former classes had been my own lack of language and inability to understand what others were saying. But now Nakagawa and Kuga were with me, and we could push ahead.

One day another man came to the door, standing there diffidently with the air of a craftsman or tradesman. He refused the first invitation to come in, but responded to the second and sat down.

'My brother sent me,' he said.

'Who is your brother?'

'He is Utsunomiya of Tomakomai. He is a Christian and he says I should become a Christian.'

Utsunomiya of Tomakomai had been a soldier with the old Japanese Imperial Army. At one time his unit had been decimated and he was one of six out of a regiment who had escaped alive. He was a wild tough man. When he was drinking, others needed to be careful that they didn't run foul of him; he also knocked his wife about quite a lot. In Tomakomai, a Swedish missionary was having tent meetings and Utsunomiya went in. He saw his own desperate need, was reminded that God had saved his life for a purpose, and came to Christ. Now he wanted his whole family to be saved, so he wrote to his younger brother and told him to find out if there was a missionary in Shizunai, and to go along. So here was Utsunomiya of Shizunai, quiet, purposeful and yet seeking.

'You had better come along on Tuesday evenings,' I said. 'There are four or five others who come then, and you can study the Bible with them. I think you will soon begin to understand it.'

Utsunomiya had been coming on Tuesdays for about a month when one evening, not a Tuesday, he called at the door. For a moment I thought he had made a mistake about the day.

'No,' he said, 'I knew it wasn't Bible class, but I have a pain in my inside.'

I wasn't used to this kind of comment, and suggested that maybe he should go to a doctor.

'Oh, no,' he said. 'It's not that kind of pain. It's a pain of sin, and I believe that you can help me cure it.'

In he came, and we talked about the way of salvation, and soon we prayed together. After this his wife and their two boys began to come along; so here was another Christian family.

What had been happening in Shizunai had also been happening in several other places where our missionaries had gone — two or three mining towns in the north, other towns along the coast, and the capital city of Hokkaido, Sapporo, now famous for Winter Olympics. At that time it was still quite a small place, but famous for its Agricultural College where Dr Clark of the United States of America had done such a lasting work. Dr Clark only came to Sapporo for six months, at the end of the nineteenth century. During that time he taught from the Bible to the boys who were studying agriculture, and as a result his whole class vowed they would follow Christ. His motto to them was 'Boys, be ambitious for Jesus Christ'. Now in the grounds of Hokkaido University in the heart of Sapporo there is a bust of Dr Clark, underneath which his motto has been significantly shortened. It reads, 'Boys, be ambitious'.

So it was at Sapporo that we decided to hold our first Christian Conference. The object was to seek God, to draw close to Him, to try to find out more about His power and His ways, to seek personal sanctification, and even for some who came to become Christians. We had never attempted anything like this before, and no one knew quite how it would work out. From Shizunai went the three high school girls, Nakagawa and Mr and Mrs Kuga, and Olga and I. Those who are used to big churches with good programmes and lively young people's meetings can't begin to understand what a fantastic joy it was for these 45 believers who came from various parts of the island to be at this Sapporo Conference. One of the high school girls said, 'I didn't realize there were so many Christians in the world'. In Acts it says that when Peter was speaking to the group at Cornelius's house, the Holy Spirit came upon them. I don't want to get into any doctrinal controversy but I think that this is what happened to the group who met together at that conference. Of course their approach to the Bible was fresh; they believed it and expected God to keep His Word. They came too with really hungry hearts, open to what God had to say to them. There was also the satisfaction of meeting others with similar experiences. So as this was all shared, there came on the one hand great personal assurance and joy in Christ, and on the other a sense of fellowship and oneness together.

The first Sunday back in Shizunai after that conference was great. There were still the same dozen or so people who had been at the Sunday meeting the week before, but what a difference! Kitajima, Sugimoto and Mikado had really been filled with the Spirit. They could not contain their joy. As they stood up one after the other to speak of what Christ had done for them, tears flowed down their cheeks. Their new-found joy and certainty in Christ showed itself in their lives: their prayer life became very real and they asked God to save the children who were coming to the Sunday School. Teaching the kids week by week wasn't a chore any more, but a real opportunity to show the children the way to God.

One day Olga picked up Mikado's Bible. It fell open and she noticed that some of the verses were underlined in red and others in blue. She said to Mikado-san, 'Do you have a special marking system?'

Mikado-san replied, 'Yes, I do'.

'What does it mean, the red and the blue?'

'Well,' she said, 'the red ones are the things I like, the blue ones are the things I don't like.'

Olga asked, 'What are you doing about it?'

'I am praying until I like all of it.'

Kitajima-san was running into the *butsudan* problem. Although we had not stressed it in our teaching, by her personal study of the Word she had come to realize that worshipping the family spirits at the shrine was wrong. Her father had died some years before, so her mother was left in the house with Kitajima-san and her elder brother. The responsibility of the daily shrine worship therefore fell upon Kitajima-san, as it usually falls on either the wife or one of the daughters. Now she had to explain to her mother that she could no longer do this. Her mother asked her if she had no concern or love for her father. Kitajima-san tried to explain to her mother that she still loved and respected her father, but she couldn't do this worship now; but the poor old lady couldn't understand. Kitajima's older brother thought her stand was pure unreasonableness, so the whole family was at loggerheads.

It didn't help the situation when Kitajima, riding on the train one day, noticed an old gentleman reading the Bible. She said to him, 'Excuse me, sir, are you a Christian?' He replied that he was. She asked him how long he had been a Christian and he replied, 'For many years'.

'Can you help me with a problem?' she asked.

'I will try to.'

'Since I have become a Christian, I have stopped worshipping at the shrine, but my family are very worried. What do you think I should do?'

The old man looked at her and smiled and said, 'Christianity is a message of love, isn't it?'

'Yes,' she said.

'In that case, if you bring trouble into your home, then you are not bringing love. On the contrary, now that you are a Christian, you ought to be the more keen to carry out worship of your ancestors. In this way you will show your Christian love.'

Poor Kitajima-san. She could see the reasonableness of this and yet she couldn't get away from the fact that the worship of spirits was idolatry and condemned by God. One of the sorrows for a missionary preaching the Gospel in a non-Christian environment is that he may well bring trouble to those who accept the message. 'Except a man take up his cross and follow me, he cannot be my disciple.' Looking back now, I see that we should have gone round to see Mrs Kitajima and tried to explain to her more fully just why her daughter was doing this.

Personality-wise Sugimoto-san was the outgoing one of the three, and now let everybody know just where she stood. In the small village where her father was head of the local primary school, she had been the leader of the young people's club. (In most Japanese towns and villages there are young people's groups which have nothing to do with religion as such, but meet together from time to time to discuss some serious subject which would not appeal to most western youngsters at all.) She got the young people's group together and told them what Christ had done for her, and as a result we were asked to go along and speak to the village. By now Okuda-san was coming up regularly from Mombetsu, taking a day off from selling fish to work with us. Kuga-sensei[1] was joining with us, and Nakagawa as he had time. So we had a team of six who could move out into the villages and take meetings as we had openings. So all of us went along to the young people's plus older people's meeting in Sugimoto's town.

It takes a lot anywhere for a young person really to stand up for Christ, but in an environment where Christ is not so well known and where Christians are few — Sugimoto was the only Christian in that village — then it really takes something. There is a basic opposition to Christianity in Japan (which may be passing now), which goes back to the old Tokugawa period about four hundred years ago. At that time, Francis Xavier began Catholic work

[1] *Sensei* means 'teacher'

down in the south of Japan, which grew among certain clans. But then came the fear that it had political overtones, and as a result there was awful persecution and Christianity as such was stamped out. It continued underground for centuries, however, and even now there are groups of people who hold to that old faith, now garbled and mixed up with all kinds of Buddhist ideas.

So we came to the village hall, and the farmers and shop keepers and children all came in together. I was thrilled that the Japanese Christians were able to proclaim Christ so clearly and so meaningfully; I hardly needed to say anything. After the meeting we had time for questions, and all sorts came. One regular chestnut at that time was, 'If America is a Christian country why did it drop the atomic bomb?' Sometimes this question was asked sincerely but at other times I think it was asked tongue in cheek. You could be awkward and say something like, 'No Pearl Harbour, no atomic bomb', but that didn't get you anywhere. I used to field this question by pointing out that there is no one Christian country, but Christians in the west do to a degree sway society; for example at the height of the bombing of Germany, leader of the church in England approached the premier and asked him if this unabated bombing was really necessary to the war effort. I was about to answer something along this line, when Mr Kuga said, 'I will answer if I may'. From our low platform he faced the upturned faces — some quizzical, some puzzled, some blank — and replied, 'Proof that America is a Christian country is that they only dropped two atomic bombs'. This stunned me. I had never thought of this approach, but the more I thought about it, the more I realized that only a Japanese could say this to a Japanese. He was saying what the others really knew, that if Japan had had this fearful weapon the militaristic authorities might not have stopped using it until they controlled the world. As a result of that meeting, we were able to begin a regular gathering in the Sugimotos' house, as well as one for the children.

Utsunomiya appeared in the *genkan* (porch) of our house one day with another man, broader than he, clad in old cavalry riding trousers and a thick windbreaker, and with a broad grin on his face. The two of them came in and he announced, 'This is my older brother'. We greeted each other bowing, and then the older brother took over, telling us that his father had recently died in his home town. To a Japanese, their home town is of vital importance. In the west you may or may not ask a person where he was born, but one of the first questions you ask a Japanese is: 'What is the place of your origin?' In every Japanese village or town there is a Buddhist temple (of course in the larger towns there may be several), and the birth of a child is registered at that temple. By this registration the child becomes a member of that particular Buddhist group. No matter where he wanders, even if he leaves the country, when he dies his body is cremated and the ashes brought back to that temple. But, even more than this, the Japanese looks back with nostalgia to the place of his birth, rather like an Irish tenor. He always speaks of returning there. Once when we were visiting in a small village in another part of Japan we met a distinguished old gentleman who had held honourable positions in the field of education, but was now living in a small house in this village, because it was his father's village and his father's house, going back nine generations. It had been his duty to return to that home. His son was a doctor, at present practising in one of the larger towns; but it was realized that at the end he too would return to his own village.

So Utsunomiya was telling me about his town Hidakamura, which was at the apex of a triangle between Tomakomai where he lived and Shizunai where his brother lived, way up in the mountains. A few weeks previously his father had died, and Utsunomiya had wanted a Christian funeral for him. He regarded this as important, because he had spoken to his father about Christ, although I can't tell whether the man really had faith or not. But before he reached home other relatives had stepped in and the Buddhist priest was there in the house. It is the custom to have the coffin in the house with a large portrait of the deceased up in front of it; and nearby some charcoal ash and joss sticks. Each friend or relative will come up, maybe put flowers in the coffin, light a joss stick and push it into the ash, and say a prayer of condolence to the photograph of the deceased. Utsunomiya felt that this was all wrong; as far as he was concerned, and as Scripture taught, the spirit of his father was now back with his Creator. He couldn't stop the Buddhist funeral, but he could make his stand. When all the preparations were ready, the priest called Utsunomiya as the oldest son to go forward and burn the joss stick. All this time he had been in a sort of daze, but at this point he suddenly stood up and said, 'No, I am not going to do this. The spirit of my father is now with his Creator. He is not here.' There was some consternation, but after the hubbub had subsided, quite a lot of people seemed interested in what he had been saying. That's why the two brothers were here in my house, asking me to go to their town for some meetings. They had hired the local hall, and I could stay with them for three days, if I would go.

I was a bit worried at this point about Mission comity. Usually missions try not to step on each other's corns. Mr Utsunomiya had been brought to the Lord by another mission, and there was an evangelist in his town. Obviously something was happening up in Hidakamura, but surely it would be better if the Japanese evangelist went? Mr Utsunomiya explained that the missionary did not feel this was the right time for the evangelist to go, because he had other work for him to do. I had often questioned the OMF policy of not employing nationals, but trusting that the Lord would raise some up to help us. This was happening, of course, with Nakagawa and Kuga and others. But here was an angle that I had not thought of — if I were holding the purse-strings, to what extent would I give freedom to an evangelist who was working with me but was dependent on the Mission for his livelihood? How much would that evangelist feel he could say to me? What sort of relationship would we have together? There was no question but that the Japanese with whom we worked were often quite blunt and direct. In fact a visiting evangelist from down south told us that in Tokyo the Japanese never told the missionary what they thought, but only what they thought he would like to hear.

'But,' he said, 'up here, they tell you the truth'.

Here was another opening, another opportunity. I took the journey to Hidakamura by bus and by train, and the three days became a week as a blizzard hit the area and we couldn't move out. Besides Utsunomiya and his brother, four other men in the district were interested in studying the Word of God, so we sat down together with the wind raging outside, and the snow coming in sudden bursts against the windows, creeping in through every crack. Every so often somebody would dash out through the door for another handful of logs and come in again with a flurry of snow, opening the front of the stove, poking the red wood coals around the log before finally pushing the log in, and then pushing the stove door shut with a clang. Old Mrs Utsunomiya served countless cups of Japanese tea. I ate raw fish, burnt fish, squid and octopus, and taught them the Word of God.

I had never seen such determination to learn. We went right through Mark's Gospel because I thought that they needed to see the life of Jesus in its entirety first. Then we started on Romans with its great doctrinal passages, right through to chapter eight. For the doctrine of the church we turned to 1 Corinthians and I aimed to show them what a church is, how it is a spiritual thing and not a building, how a group of men with the Spirit of God who come together in fellowship constitute a church in its simplest form. They thrived on it. Our sleeping arrangements were simple. Hudson Taylor had urged his missionaries to live as closely to the people as possible. Old Mrs Utsunomiya laid down six mattresses side by side and threw several over-mattresses onto them. The pillows were a kind of bag filled with hard beans. Then we all seven piled in in our underclothes, and grandma came and tucked us in. I remember thinking before going off to sleep, 'I can't be closer to the national than this'. Ten years earlier four of the men had been in the Japanese army — enemies. That was God's purpose for the beginning of the church in that town. Later the evangelist did go up and his mission took over the work.

All this time, I was having my own battle between faith and doubt, between belief that God could work and frustration with some of our methods. I remember one evening being very vocal about all the things that the Mission had done wrong. Olga listened patiently for some time and then said, 'Why don't you write down on a piece of paper some of the things which the Mission has done for you?' So I wrote them down. In a sense the Mission had enabled me to fulfil my calling of coming overseas to preach the Gospel. There had been my fare to the field; there had been the money involved in language study, payment of teachers and so on; there was the monthly payment of rent and the money for food and our remittance, and in addition to this, there was a worldwide fellowship of prayer of which I was part. When we had asked for a tent the previous summer, Headquarters had recognized this need and had advanced funds for it. As I went through some of these positive things, I began to get a more balanced outlook.

12
A FRUITFUL TIME

GOD WORKS THROUGH people, ordinary people, when they give themselves to Him. The followers of Jesus were very ordinary people, fishermen and so on. But they learned from Him and lived with Him and so, when they were filled with His Spirit, God was able to do great things through them. In the kind of thing we were trying to do, both in Shizunai and along the coast with other missionaries, I could see two principles. The first was that we had got to work at it. The Bible says, 'He who sows sparingly will reap sparingly'. For this reason Olga and I were always trying to get out to reach people.

We were still having to spend up to three hours every morning in language study, and I don't think our Japanese friends understood why we were doing this or what it cost us. They would drop in for a chat, and we'd like that; we certainly didn't want to give the impression of being too busy for them. We had made one mistake along that line. One afternoon when I was out with my tracts and booklets, I got talking with three young men working at a filling station. They were a bit shy of the foreigner at first, but gradually they thawed as we talked, leaning against a truck, their overalls streaked with oil. The conversation wasn't too spiritual at times;

they were interested in what foreign girls were like. I gave them some booklets and said, 'Why don't you come round and visit me sometime?'

'Where do you live?'

'I'll draw you a map,' and I fished out a pencil from my tract bag and drew on the back of a tract. 'This is the address; you can see it on the back of this leaflet. This leaflet tells you all about the true God.' I could see them grin sheepishly when I mentioned that.

When I got back to the house I mentioned the incident to Olga. A few nights later I was feeling groggy after an injection, and had to leave for Tokyo on the 5.30 am train. So I went to bed about quarter to eight. At ten past eight I heard Olga talking to somebody in the *genkan* (porch). Then they went away.

'Who was that?'

'That was those three lads you talked to at the filling station. I told them you had had an injection and were feeling groggy, so you had gone to bed.'

'I suppose they'll come back some other time.'

But they never did come back. I don't suppose they believed for a moment that what Olga had said was true: they presumed that the foreigner had lost interest in them. If I had struggled up, put on my dressing gown and gone out to talk with them for a bit, they would have seen that Olga was telling the truth, and after a few minutes they would have gone away quite happily.

I suppose subconsciously we divided people into three. First of all there were those who had no interest in the Gospel and maybe never would have, but nevertheless had a right to know that Christ had died for them. These could be reached in all kinds of ways, and one of the chief ones was by distributing tracts. In the town there were several small factories employing twenty to thirty men, and the foreman would usually let me in to talk to the men and give them some tracts. We could also put Gospel leaflets in the newspaper, which would then be distributed all round the town. We reached out by street preaching and tent preaching too. Then there were those who had some interest, though we were never quite sure what the interest was about. It may have just been in the shape of our noses! But they were prepared to invite us into their homes or come along to ours. And then of course there were the real Christians.

You could divide people by age too. The children were great, always prepared to be friendly and to listen. In the old days in Japan, there was a lively character known as the *kamishibai* man. *Kami* means paper and *shibai* means theatre, so it is literally 'paper theatre'. This fellow used to travel around the town on a bicycle with a square frame at the back, especially during the children's holiday time. Into this frame he would drop a series of pictures one at a time, and at the same time he told the story. He would gesture, shout, or lower his voice in a conspiratorial whisper; his two fingers would come out to lift the next picture from the back, to be placed over the front one in the frame; the children would stand round ready to cheer the hero or groan at the villain, and when the show was all over the *kamishibai* man would sell them a kind of powdery sweet stuff at double the price it was worth. Of course they had had the story and been entertained for half an hour or so. Somebody had got the bright idea of adopting this method for Bible stories, and so we had *Kamishibai* Bible stories. As well as this way of reaching the children there was the regular Sunday School, and classes for middle school and high school youngsters.

After a morning struggling with Japanese characters, vocabulary and grammatical construction, I was ready for my *oyako*. After dinner I would stretch out on the *tatami* flooring with a folded *zabuton* as my pillow and close my eyes. One day there came a rattle at the door and a call! I pushed open the inner door and there was a very interesting figure. His feet were clad in a kind of slipper which freed the big toe. His trousers were like riding breeches — they were tight to the leg, but blossomed out round the seat. His rather grimy shirt was covered by a robe which looked more like an old bedsheet flung across his left shoulder. In one hand he had a drum which was really just a skin pulled tight over a twelve-inch frame, hanging from his shoulder was a long bag, and in his other hand he had a little drum-stick. It was my old acquaintance the Nichiren priest.

Nichiren is Japanese Buddhism; it claims to be the only true way, which is unique — other Buddhists give plenty of room for what everybody else believes. It is the laymen's movement of Nichiren, called Sookagakkai, which has had such an impact on Japanese society in the last couple of decades and now has its own political party, with quite a lot of seats in parliament.

I invited the priest in, and we sat near the window where every passerby could see Buddhist travelling mendicant and Christian missionary in cheerful conversation together. This worried me a bit because after his previous visits some of the neighbours had said it was great that Nichiren and Christianity could get together — after all, all religions were the same. Still, it wasn't my intention to be awkward this time. We exchanged the usual comments about the weather and the latest news, and then began to talk about Christ and Nichiren. Nichiren, well-known in Japanese history, was in many ways a reformer calling people to a more simple way of life. At that time the Chinese were coming to attack Japan with a great navy. According to tradition, in answer to the nation's repentance and Nichiren's prayer there was a great storm and the Chinese navy was wrecked. It was the wind of God, from which the word *kamikaze* has come.

When I spoke of the resurrection of Christ, the priest retaliated by saying that Nichiren also rose from the dead, for Nichiren had been under the death sentence and was about to be executed when at the last moment he was reprieved. As mentally Nichiren had already given up life, this was the same as resurrection. Then we turned to the character of God. 'God is love,' I said. The priest, suddenly angry, retorted, 'If God is love, why did He leave

His Son Jesus to die on the cross? Why didn't He rescue Him?' I replied with some feeling, 'Because on the cross Jesus Christ was dying for your sin'. Then the priest became really angry. He jumped to his feet, walked up and down our room with rapid steps two or three times, flung open with a crash the door into our porch, slipped on his shoes, grabbed his drumstick and other accoutrements and fled down the road. He never came back.

The second principle we saw in our work was that we could do nothing of ourselves. A politician or an advertising man can convince people how to vote or what to buy even against their will but it isn't like that with the work we do for God. It is obvious when you think about it because Christianity isn't just a system of belief, it's a new life; and until God hands out the new life, then people are dead. So there's the paradox that we are to preach the Gospel to everybody, go out on the highways and byways to compel them to come in; and yet we know that all this isn't going to count for anything unless God works. I've not really been able to work out the relationship between our concern to see people come to Christ, the amount of prayer we put into it, and how God answers. Still, I think there is enough in the Bible for us to get down on our knees and plead with God for blessing. The Word says, 'Not by might, nor by power, but by My Spirit, says the Lord'. In another place He says, 'I will pour out water on him who is thirsty'. Then there is the story of how concerned the disciples were after Peter and John had been ill-treated. In some ways it's a bit ironical, because it looks as if the disciples weren't so concerned about the hard time Peter and John were getting, as that they might stop preaching the resurrection! These disciples knew that they had no pull with government, or prestige in society, but they reckoned they knew God Who had the power. That was a mighty prayer meeting which changed things considerably, and the answer was in the coming of the Holy Spirit.

Olga and I knew that we had the Holy Spirit; we looked to be filled with the Holy Spirit. What we longed for and pleaded with God for was His Holy Spirit to come in with power on the work we were doing. We searched our own motives, and as far as we could see we weren't looking for success for ourselves. We were just angry that the devil seemed to have all the power, and Jesus wasn't getting the glory to which He was entitled.

Praise the Lord! Since just before Christmas there were signs that God was with us. Sunday mornings, starting at half past eight, the children began to pile into our front room. Mikado-san and Sugimoto-san, together with Olga, taught these youngsters regularly the most important things that anybody could ever learn. When they had gone, we pushed the benches round, put away the flannelgraph material and brought out the music stand and Olga's violin. At about 10.30 the nine or so keen Christians were coming in for morning service. There were surprises too in those morning meetings. I saw a man come in and sit at the back one day, but I couldn't remember who he was. We had a kind of elongated apple box which we had painted and made into a small pulpit, and as I stood behind this and preached I looked at him every so often. After the service I beckoned to Mr Kuga, 'Ask that new young man his name and where he has come from'. Kuga went quietly across to him, bowed and introduced himself and they talked for a few minutes, then Kuga came back and grinned.

'He says you know him well.' I was struggling desperately in my mind, wondering where I had seen him. Was it in one of the other small group meetings along the coast? Was he the son of some family I had visited? I shook my head.

'How do I know him? Or how does he know me?' I asked.

'Well, he says you met him about a year ago on the train. You gave him a tract and he has kept it ever since. As it's got your address on the back, he has come here today.' I suppose I was the only foreigner he had ever met, so he had remembered me well; but I had long forgotten him.

The Christians were beginning to think about summer evangelism and short-bearded Ega-san, his face split in a wide grin, suggested a meeting to discuss it. So here we were in our back room, sitting crouched round the low table. I was deliberately as negative as possible. If we were to do any tent work this coming summer, I wanted the burden to be shared by my Japanese friends equally with Olga and myself. We bowed our heads for a time of prayer, and one or two of our friends asked the Lord to guide us. Then we opened our eyes and looked at one another. I noticed that Mr Kuga, as befitting a high school teacher, was the only one wearing a tie.

'We have come here to talk about summer evangelism. What is the point of tent work? You know that Mr Hayman and I and Mr Lee, the Chinese man, tried tent meetings last summer and they came to nothing.'

Ega-san leaned forward, his face suddenly serious, his hands pressing on his knees. 'We have a command from God. Whether the people believe or whether they do not believe, we should tell them. We should have a summer tent meeting in this town.'

I raised more difficulties. 'Who is going to preach? I cannot carry eight days of preaching. My Japanese is not sufficient.' As Olga said afterwards, it was a bit disconcerting the way they agreed with that remark! The discussion became general and animated.

'We could get an evangelist, couldn't we?'

'Who would pay his fare to come a distance?'

'We could look after his fare, couldn't we, and of course he'd need a gift too.'

'Where would he live? He'd have to have a room to himself for a week or so.' Mr Kuga, looking across at his wife as she nodded in agreement, said, 'We have a small room. It's full of lumber, but we could push it on one side. There'd be room for him there.'

I tried not to show my emotions. God was good! In just a few short months He had brought together this group of men and women and touched their hearts, and they wanted Shizunai and the coast to know of the Lord. I also wondered, as the talk went on, whether they had had a little private meeting before coming to our house. I threw out a feeler.

'Where would we get an evangelist from? Do you know of anybody?' The talking died down and there was quiet for a moment. Mr Kuga, looking round at the others, suggested, 'How about Mr Noguchi?' The way they all nodded their smiling assent made me suspect even more that there had been some agreement beforehand, and I nodded assent too.

* * * * *

It is strange how you meet people. I recalled a bright autumn day before Olga and I were married, when I was living with David Hayman in Kutchan. Language study had gone sour on me and I had decided to go out for a long walk, probably all day. I walked along the mountain paths, gulping in deep breaths of air, and felt really great. There wasn't a cloud in the sky; the sun was warm on my back and nature looked beautiful. Farm houses along the way were usually two or three hundred yards off the main road, and so I would make a detour along the cart tracks into the farm yard to offer Christian books. Usually everybody was out in the field working, except for old grandma, and it always amused me when she said 'There's nobody here,' thinking herself unworthy of recognition, or hoping that the foreigner wouldn't notice her. Some people were happy to stop and talk for a bit, though one or two were a bit startled at the foreigner appearing from nowhere, and one man even warned me that I needed to be careful of the sun; it might affect my head.

So I walked all the morning till I came to the village of Kunikami. Small dark-haired, dark-eyed heads were turned wonderingly in my direction and I fished in my bag for some children's tracts and offered one. A boy click-clacked in his wooden sandals toward me, snatched it and went back to his friends. Then their fears were overcome and they were round me, chattering and laughing at my accent, taking the literature. I didn't notice a man approaching until he said to me, 'Are you a Christian?' When I said I was he said he was too, and invited me to come back to the house with him. He asked me if I had eaten and I said I hadn't, so his wife busied herself making something for me, and in the meantime I went fast asleep on the floor! They must have let me sleep for an hour or more before I opened my eyes. He was a member of a church in Iwanai, where the fire had been on the night of the typhoon, and worked in the sulphur mines which were the economic mainstay of the village. He told me that ever since the war years he had had a Sunday School in his house to teach children, and also a meeting for older people, and asked me to come along and speak sometime. This became a custom and I used to go out from Kutchan by bus about once a month.

One Sunday morning I had arrived early and was sitting with my Japanese Bible on my knees, looking up a few words in my Japanese dictionary. The room I was in was *tatami* of course, very simply furnished; a well-worn chest of drawers was up against the wall with a handle missing from the top right-hand drawer, and some Japanese dolls and a *kimono*-clad dancing girl in a glass case on top; a small low table about eighteen inches in height and another little table with a radio on it were the only other items of furniture. The villagers came in with their little bundles, the coloured handkerchief-like *furoshiki* with Bible and hymnbook wrapped up in it. As they greeted each other, took out their Bibles and hymnbooks, I noticed perched above the door a picture of Christ. Of course in Mr Narumi's house there was no godshelf and no ancestor shrine. Mr Narumi saw me looking at the picture and explained, 'We Japanese like to have something we can see, something we can look at'. How does this fit in with God's commands about having no man-made thing to worship? To what extent do you compromise with the culture? The Japanese usually keep a picture of the dead in the ancestor shrine, which is prominently displayed at certain times of the year. One church I knew of catered to this by having pictures of the Japanese Christians who had died brought along to the church on resurrection Sunday.

Among the half a dozen believers that day, there was one young man whom I had not met before, and Mr Narumi introduced me to him. He was a small thin man with an unusually sharp nose for a Japanese, intense eyes and a pale complexion.

'This is Mr Noguchi. He is from Kyuushuu.' I bowed, leaning forward with my hands on the *tatami*.

'Mr Noguchi is interested in one of the young ladies here and we are arranging a *miai*.' '*Mi*' is part of the verb *miru* which means to look, and '*ai*' is the root of *au* which is to meet. So *miai* means literally 'looking and meeting'. Even today the greatest percentage of weddings in Japan are arranged in this way. The middleman is usually the manager of the office in which the bridegroom-to-be works, or the foreman in his workshop, or the headmaster of his school. The middleman's responsibilities do not end after .the wedding; when the first quarrel begins, then the middleman is called in to a family discussion to help sort things out.

I met Noguchi-sensei here and there after that Sunday in Kunikami. He was present at that first winter conference in Sapporo where our high school girls from Shizunai had really got on fire for the Lord. And this was the man the believers wanted to invite for a week of meetings. I was more than pleased at the prospect and this summer we would once again get the Gospel out along the coast. We would be preaching and teaching and giving out literature and putting up posters, taking the tent up and down . . . but there was missionary help for Olga and me on the way.

Lionel Thomson was an Australian, a man of tremendous energy, a gifted evangelist. He had had a struggle with the language, but with a few sentences was able to bring people to the point of decision. When he came to Shizunai we found him a little room in the home of a man in the truck business, just across the way from us. I liked this truck owner and we often talked together, but he never showed any interest in the Gospel. He had been captured by the Russians in Manchuria after the war, and when he was released the government gave him a bit of help to start again in Hokkaido. He had worked hard and by now had bought three or four trucks. Being across the way from us, he had been one of the first I visited when we moved in; later he paid us a visit and we talked further. He surprised me once by asking, 'What do you think of Adam Smith's "Wealth of Nations"?' Fortunately I had heard about this book and was able to make some sort of comment, although I had never read it. The Japanese are rather like this, and have all sorts of odd areas of information. They get an interest in some particular person in Western history and make a real study of him.

So when Lionel Thomson arrived he lived in the room across the way and had meals with us. I don't know how other Missions work, but the OMF pools all its resources quarterly and then shares the money out. Some money is obviously well earmarked already, such as fares to and from the fields, and rent for all the houses in which the hundreds of missionaries are living in almost all of the countries of Asia. The Mission also supplies furniture. Then there are all kinds of other expenses like radio, travel, literature, language study and so on. Money is also allocated to each centre for food, gas and heating. Along this line we had an interesting answer to prayer, which shows that God hears and answers even in the small areas. Lionel had an appetite that went along with his terrific energy, and Olga was a bit nonplussed about having to satisfy it. Just about then a friend from the country began calling with big chunks of mutton or lamb. We never did discover where he was getting it from, but it met the need for some months.

Now Lionel was with us, we could step up the whole programme. He learned the children's choruses, and would tap the beat out with his feet so that the floor swayed and Olga's music on the violin-stand was flipped farther and farther along until it fell on the floor. The children enjoyed every minute of it. More and more openings along the coast were coming, and Lionel and Nakagawa and I did more street preaching, house meetings and tract distribution. Lionel was a good man to pray with too.

So came the night before the Shizunai campaign was to begin. That afternoon the tent had been brought up from the shed and taken to the site, its walls and roof unrolled, its guy ropes unwound and laid out, a tent peg to every guy rope. The long poles were joined together; two of us stood by the long guy ropes at each end of the tent, and the other three stood under the canvas and lifted the tent up to the point where the other two could pull it upright. At this point a couple of us dashed out to take the ropes from the other side of the tent to keep it from falling again. Stakes were driven in, the walls laced up and Gospel posters pinned round the walls. All this was becoming so familiar that we could almost do it in our sleep.

Thin pale Noguchi-sensei was met at the railway station by Kuga, the high school teacher, and brought straight to the prayer meeting. When I talked to Noguchi-sensei years afterwards about that meeting, he said his reaction had been that the power was in the church; our reaction had been that the power was in the visiting evangelist. The truth was that it wasn't in either: the Lord visited His people. We sang a few hymns from an old Japanese hymnbook which has a lot of Christian songs that stress the cross and the blood and the resurrection, and the personal work of the Holy Spirit in the believer. Noguchi-sensei then opened his Bible and prayed in quiet urgent tones before he began to speak to us. I suppose there were fifteen or sixteen of us in the room, and apart from old Ega the Ainu and Nakagawa the boxer, all the Japanese believers were people who had come to us since the summer before. So to them tent evangelism was a new thing. Noguchi talked about the cross and about the necessity of being filled with the Spirit; then he went on further to talk about the need for an anointing of the Spirit of God for this particular service, this period of tent evangelism in Shizunai. There wasn't anything profound in what he said; he spoke quietly and very quickly, sometimes serious, sometimes his face lighting up with a quick smile, and after about thirty minutes or so he closed his Bible and looked up at us. 'Maybe there are one or two who would like to pray,' he said.

I wish I could describe the feeling in the room. Perhaps we didn't look very attractive, but we knew that we were saved, and we knew that God had called us to witness for Him. We knew that we had an enemy and that he wanted to destroy our faith. We knew that we couldn't do anything ourselves, but that God would work for us if we asked Him. One after another, with no waiting between, the believers poured out their hearts to God for the people of Shizunai, for courage to witness, for power through the preaching of God's word. Some confessed sin and coldness of heart, and appeared to receive forgiveness as their prayer turned from repentance to the joy of acceptance.

Then one girl began to pray something like this, 'God, for six months I have been reading your Word and listening to preaching, reading books about Christianity, and I have talked to these Christians here, but I can't get to you.' Her prayer trailed off as she began to sob. I was a bit embarrassed and didn't quite know what to do, but old Ega said to her, 'Trust in the Lord Jesus Christ and you shall be saved'.

She replied, 'It's no good just believing. I need to know that God has heard my prayer. I need to know His presence.' The room was quiet as Ega said to me, 'Go across and put your hands on her'. I had never done this before and I didn't want to do it now, but she was getting quite worked up, so I went across and put my hands on her and prayed the words of John 3.16. 'For God so loved the world that He gave His only begotten Son, that whosoever believes in Him should not perish but have everlasting life.' I chose this verse because it was the only one I was sure I'd remember right through to the end in Japanese. I seemed to be supported by the prayers of the others, as I asked God to give this girl eternal life and to give her understanding that she had it. In a moment she relaxed and became full of joy, she was praising the Lord and so were we all. We began to sing spontaneously 'The Holy Spirit has come'. Yes, God the Holy Spirit had come right down into that meeting, and had shown us victory through the power of prayer in Christ. He had made us into one body, and we knew the victory had been won.

Every night for a week the tent was filled, first with children and then with adults. Noguchi preached simply in his quiet matter-of-fact way, but the Holy Spirit was working, breaking up the fallow ground. Every night after the meeting there were seven, eight or a dozen enquirers, and the young Christians with their Bibles open were answering questions, showing the way of salvation and praying with the enquirers. There were 47 decisions for Christ that week, and afterwards 25-30 people came along regularly to the Sunday morning meeting. God had used us and heard our prayers, not because of anything in us but because He was pleased to do so.

That September, in a small hut in our Superintendent's garden, Grace our daughter was born at one o'clock in the morning. I was sleeping in the Super's house and Dr Roslyn Hayman called me across. Olga was sitting up in the bed with the baby nestling in her arms. The hut was very warm and I felt as if the room was going round me. Olga said to Roslyn, 'You'd better get him a chair and give him a cup of tea'.

13
CUSHIONS AND CULTURE

WHEN YOU LOOK back you can often see that significant things have come out of almost casual conversations. One day David Hayman and I were standing in our swimming trunks on the beach at Takayama. The lifeguard was watching the antics of a number of children in the shallows, and a game of volley ball was going on behind us. The sun was hot on our shoulders so we moved across to the shade of the overhanging cliff. David had been Japan Field Superintendent for about eight years and was soon to go on furlough. The Super's job is to look after missionaries. He is both personnel manager and pastor, which really makes the job well-nigh impossible. Yet without both responsibilities perhaps the job is not worth having! He spends quite a bit of time travelling and visiting missionaries, talks over with them their hopes, their plans and their methods, and helps them along.

Glancing up at the overhanging cliffs, David remarked that he would not be at 'Tak' next year because he was due for furlough in Australia. 'Who do you think I should recommend to do the Super's job while I'm away?' he said, and went on to mention three names. I did not answer him immediately because I was thinking the names over, and couldn't see what those chaps had on me! At least if it was only for a year. As though reading my mind, David said bluntly, 'You don't think you could do it, do you?' David was nothing if not frank. I stated a little peevishly, 'If it was only for a year I wouldn't mind having a go at it,' and there the matter dropped. Normally a Superintendent was chosen by Headquarters in Singapore in those days, after getting the recommendations of senior field missionaries. But when a Super was on furlough another man was asked to fill in without the formality of getting the missionaries to vote on him.

In the event, there was a whole change in administration. David, before he went on furlough, was made a Director for OMF work in Japan and Korea, and the OMF members on the Japan field asked for David Michell, now Home Director for Canada, to be the Japan Super. That was a very popular choice, and I had no grumbles about it.

At this time Olga and I were living in the city of Hirosaki, the county town of Aomori Province at the northern end of the long island of Honshu. It was an ancient city with a mediaeval castle on the heights in the centre. By this time we had three children, two of whom were at OMF's Chefoo School in Nanae, Hokkaido, so we only saw them at holiday times. Our youngest was still with us. Our house was an old-style building with sliding doors dividing the rooms. In the summer we could push the outside wall at the rear right back, so that the whole of the house was open to the sun.

OMF missionaries had been living for some time

in Hirosaki, and as a result a church had been formed. The believers felt they could support a pastor so Mr Nakano, a quiet young man with an even quieter wife and two small children, was invited. As there was no church building, the believers rented a house for the pastor and his family which was also used for worship meetings. The pastor and the believers asked OMF if Olga and I could go and work with him, and so began a new stage of our education in Japanese culture. Up until now we had been in what we called pioneer church-planting, where the missionary was of course the leader. As most of the believers were new converts and had no idea of what the church was all about, they were content to let it be so. A Japanese pastor was a different kettle of fish. We began in no time to see where he thought the priorities lay.

Japanese culture, we discovered, consists of groups. The two main pressure groups are the family and the business, in other words your relatives and your company. Let's take the company. Hours are nine to five but nobody is going to leave that office until the Chief leaves it. And the Chief is not going to leave for another hour at least, because that would show his insincerity. The claims of these two groups, the business and the family, often pull a man in two different directions all his life. In one situation the company's claim may be stronger than the wife's; but in another situation — a son's graduation, for example — family may come before business. Sometimes the two groups overlap, as when the manager of a local bank is asked by a family to find a wife for their son who is working in the bank. The manager would regard this as quite a normal request; in fact he would expect it.

A third kind of pressure group is what you might call the vertical relationship. A person who has been through university or high school will look at others from that college as senior or junior to him, according to their position above or below him. So he will either show them appropriate respect, or expect such respect.

It was quite a time before we understood that in becoming a Christian a person then experiences a fourth pressure group, for the Church is a pressure group which makes demands on the Christian's time and behaviour. One day Mr Nakano and I had been going through the English version of a few verses of the Bible. Although he knew very little English he was quite excited, because the English seemed much clearer than the Japanese. Then he turned to me to say that he had to take an evangelistic trip to Tokyo. I didn't know if he was pulling my leg — his face was quite straight. 'But who are you preaching for? Where are you speaking?' I asked.

'I am not doing any preaching. I am going to look for husbands for two of the young ladies in the church,' he said, telling me their names. 'You will realize that as Christians they cannot marry unbelievers. But their parents are not Christians, so it's up to me to find them young men from the churches in Tokyo. In this way their families will realize that the Church is sincere, and their hearts will be open to the Gospel. So, this is evangelism!' I saw what he meant!

When a Christian young couple get married, it isn't the families of the couple that get involved but the Church, which starts planning six months before. Committees are formed and every last contingency is foreseen and planned for. When Mr and Mrs Watanabe, a young hairdresser and permanent wave specialist, were married, every detail was decided and noted and the person informed, down to who would put the plug in the socket to turn on the electric guitar when the Hawaiian band started playing Christian songs. My Japanese friends want to know where they are going, and to them our apparently casual approach to life borders on the 'insincere'.

It was in this area of the casual approach that my friend Pastor Nakano and I began to have problems. Although Japanese culture is a vertical one, that is to say someone is the boss, and although I was older than he, I was determined not to be that boss. At the same time, he was finding it quite difficult to know how to deal with me because of his own hangups and cultural background. For example, on Thursdays he had a home meeting at the house of one of the older Christians, Mr Tanaka, who worked for the Post Office and had turned to Christ through hearing Christian radio programmes. The meeting consisted regularly of just Mr and Mrs Tanaka and Pastor Nakano, seated at a low table in their small room. It did not occur to me to go to that meeting, and if I had so thought I would immediately have dismissed the idea — not that I despised the meeting, but I reckoned it didn't need two brothers there to encourage Mr and Mrs Tanaka. I could be better used visiting other homes of friends and inquirers, of whom I had plenty.

Mr Nakano and I were walking one day through the grounds of the old castle looking at the massive wooden gates protected by heavy metal. The cherry blossom was beginning to fall from the trees, always a significant moment for the Japanese. Mr Nakano obviously had something on his mind and without looking at me said, 'You have a problem with the Tanakas?' Quite puzzled, I said I had the warmest regard for them.

'Do you oppose the meeting at the Tanakas' house?'

I was getting even more mystified, but assured him that I was all in favour. 'Then,' he said in a bewildered voice, 'why don't you attend it?'

He went on to explain that in the eyes of a believer my non-attendance at a church meeting, as a Christian worker, would be interpreted as either insincerity or to mean that I had some problem with the pastor or with the Tanakas.

Olga was running into the same kind of trouble the other way round. She had been asked to take charge of the women's meeting. Knowing that Mrs Nakano, though a friendly soul, was not very fit and had two small children to care for, she was glad to do it. The first time she led the meeting the pastor came too, and she thought this was to make her feel at home. But he kept coming every week, and at the end of the meeting he would say the benediction. Through this we learned that the pastor of a Japanese church has to be at every meeting, no matter who is running it, otherwise he is regarded as insincere.

Working with Mr Nakano, I could see that he wasn't a dictator. So why did he have this attitude? Thinking about it, I began to realize how difficult the position of a Japanese pastor is. In the west, even though there may be all kinds of comments made about ministers or vicars, we know their place in society. But to the Japanese a Christian pastor is a strange phenomenon. They know what a Buddhist priest's position is, or a Shinto priest's, but cannot understand the Christian pastor's. The nearest context they can find for him is that of the old-time 'teacher', who might be a teacher of judo or wisdom or philosophy. The teacher taught; the pupils listened. So the pastor teaches and the believers listen.

One day Olga received a letter from a gentleman in Kitami, about which she got quite excited. She had lived in Kitami before we were married, while doing her initial language study. This old man, Mr Shibakawa, wanted her to go to the City Hospital in Hirosaki, where she would find a young woman, the daughter of an old friend of his, working in the office. (Another example of the pressure of relationships.) Old Mr Shibakawa asked Olga to lead the young woman to Christ, as she had many problems. She dutifully went along to the hospital and found a rather shy young lady working there. Olga explained who she was and why she had come, and very soon they became friends. Olga brought her to church and introduced her to Mr Nakano, and later she did indeed believe in Christ and was baptized. Both at the time and afterwards we were very impressed by the pastoral care and concern that the minister showed, but were mystified that he had known about the lady but had made no approach to her on his own initiative, not even asking a Christian woman to visit her.

Relationships are so important. My old friend Mr Nakagawa, the boxer, taught me something else along this line. Many years after we first knew each other, Nakagawa invited me to take some evangelistic meetings in his church in Shikoku, down south, and I was glad to do so. He talked over with me some of his pastoral problems. For example, as a result of a misunderstanding a young couple had not been to church for some time. It was obviously more than time for the pastor to make some move, and I asked Nakagawa if he had visited them. He said he hadn't, but had phoned them. I got quite heated. 'Man, you ought to get round and see them,' I said warmly. Then Nakagawa explained to me that the problem was that they were not really 'his people' — by this he meant that he had not actually baptized them, because they had come from another church. They had only been coming to his church for a couple of years. In Nakagawa's mind this put him at a disadvantage in trying to heal the breach.

It took me a long time to understand the importance of the annual church meeting. Although society is vertical and apparently dictatorial, there is a place where it is absolutely democratic. Somewhere in every organization — whether family or business — there is a place and time for everyone to have his say and be given a fair hearing. In the church this is at the annual church meeting. There the things which are decided become the law of the Medes and Persians for the following year, and not even the pastor can change anything without permission from the whole group of believers. One of the matters that perplexed young Japanese pastors who took over groups of believers from us was that we had very little in the way of records of what had happened in the past, and we certainly had no record of annual general meetings. We missionaries had just got on with the job, and that with a minimum of administration.

It was at a church annual meeting that I ran up against one important priority in Japanese culture. In fact it was at a meeting to decide the agenda for the annual meeting that I heard the word *bochi*. I knew what it meant but I could not see its relevance to us — a small party of believers with a lot to be done, film evangelism, personal work, instruction of inquirers, baptismal courses . . . why drag in burial grounds? Yes, this is what the word *bochi* means — a burial ground. Yet hardly a burial ground because the Japanese do not bury their dead but cremate them. After some relative has carefully identified the ashes they put them into small urns, and a *bochi* is a small tract of land with a plain stone building where the urns of the dead can be placed.

It is very hard even for Japanese Christians to get away from the religious belief in the need to placate the spirits of the dead — it has such a long history. No spirit likes to think of the ashes of his old body not being cared for. The Buddhist priest understands this problem. There was an old priest who looked after a temple in the south of Japan during the war, quite near to some mines where prisoners of war, British, American and others, were forced to work. Many died during that period, and this old priest made every effort to get the ashes of these prisoners, or a photograph or identity disc. He would keep them in his temple and pray for the souls of the dead. I believe that after the war he even made some attempt to contact their relatives. It was dangerous for him to care for the enemy in this way, and at one time the military came and questioned him about his patriotism. He looked them straight in the face and told them he was about his business, let them get about theirs. They left the temple in a hurry.

So now this small fellowship of believers, as yet without pastor or building, were already thinking about a place for the ashes of their members. It was pointed out to me that any middle-aged person who had not yet accepted Christ would be helped by knowing that Christians had a place for the ashes. The *bochi* was removing a cultural hang-up for inquirers — it was pre-evangelism! To what extent has evangelism been slowed down in the past by our apparent lack of thoughtfulness?

The early morning sun had not yet begun to melt the ridge of snow on the fence when Pastor Nakano arrived on our doorstep in what for him was an agitated state of mind.

'We've got to move — the owner wants his house and has a buyer for it.'

We invited him in and he slipped off his shoes, by pressing one heel against the other with a downward movement that he must have practised from the time he could walk. He stepped up onto our raised inner porch and into the blue slippers Olga had hurriedly selected from the rack at the side, then pushing the slippers off as he stepped into the *tatami*-floored living room. Olga, herself in a kneeling position, pushed a small square cushion towards him with both hands. He ignored this, kneeling beside it in a formal fashion. I begged him to be at ease and he sat with crossed legs on the flat cushion.

With formalities over we could get down to business. Pastor Nakano observed ruefully that in the couple of years he had worked with us, he and his family had had to move seven times. Apart from the effect on his family — for in some cases his children had had to change schools — it was no way to build up a church. 'We have got to get our own building.' he said.

We asked three other leading Christians to come round and talk over the problem. Later the other believers would be told about it. Katagawa-san arrived first; the Christian bookstore he ran was just around the corner. Some years before he had been in hospital with TB, and friends had brought

Christian books for him to read. He had ignored them at first but out of boredom one day he began to read one, and then the Bible. A few days later he slipped from the sheets to the floor and, kneeling beside his hospital bed, accepted Christ as his Saviour. Katagawa had dedicated his life and gifts to God in Christian literature and had been in bookshop work ever since. He had rather a big nose for a Japanese, and was very aware of this. On one occasion when he and I had been out together, a Japanese complimented me on my use of the language and then turned to compliment Katagawa, who insisted in a complaining voice 'I am Japanese'.

The next to arrive was a talented music teacher who, being a lady, had to be asked three times to accept the proffered cushion. Mr Itoh, who had been converted while in a mental hospital, was the third, and then we got down to discussion. The pastor outlined the problem and what he felt was the solution. The next questions, of course were, 'How much will it cost?' 'How much money do we have?'

Pastor Nakano didn't look happy. Although we had had a 'building fund' for some time, the believers had not taken it very much to heart, and we needed seventy times as much as we had just to pay for a piece of land. As we prayed together the conviction grew almost minute by minute that the next step for the church was, in spite of the problems, to find land, buy it and look for a way of building. And the rest of the believers were equally at one in this decision. The weeks and months that followed were times of testing as well as triumph. There were times when Pastor Nakano felt that he almost stood alone as others began to despair. There were other times when there was a fellowship in sharing, like the jumble sale. Olga and I were not too happy about the jumble sale. Back in England in Poole, I had consistently opposed jumble sales, feeling they did not reflect the way God supplies in answer to prayer. However, here in Hirosaki I wasn't in charge. Katagawa-san visited the American Army Base in Misawa with some of his books, and the Chaplain there remarked that he had a lot of clothes, some hardly used, that he wanted to get rid of. Katagawa mentioned the jumble sale and pretty soon every bit of space in the Nakanos' house and ours was filled with large cardboard cartons. I do not think that the sale realized much in real cash, but I was interested in the way the activity stirred up and excited the believers, because they were doing something together and doing it for the Lord. Gradually the pile of clothing disappeared. What the small-framed inhabitants of Hirosaki who bought the clothing ever did with the large American-style garments I never did know. What I do know is that a few weeks later the American Chaplain dropped in and settled into a chair while we served him coffee. We did not inflict the cushion on the floor on him! 'Ya'know something?' he said, 'I should never have let you have those clothes. They were supposed to be for an American charity. Never mind, it's too late now. We can get some more.'

Pastor Nakano spent a lot of time going around looking for land. One day he found a farmer who said he would sell him some, and at a lower price than usual. One of the OMF missionaries, an architect who had never expected to use his training in Japan, drew up the plans. Then on Sunday morning the pastor announced an anonymous gift from a doctor in the town. It was a very large sum indeed and I couldn't help wondering what the pastor had let himself in for — what sort of responsibility would Mr Nakano feel that he had towards this man after receiving such a gift. At the entrance to his house I waited a bit while other visitors slipped into their shoes and left. Then I asked him, 'Pastor Nakano, who gave you all the money?'

'I am afraid I cannot tell you that, except that the man is not a Christian but he does want to see Christian work grow.'

I pressed him again. 'Have you put yourself or the church under any obligation in accepting this money?' Obligation can have dire complications in Japan. Pastor Nakano assured me that it was all in order, and I never learned where the money came from. This kind of gift encouraged the believers to give sacrificially, but it was still a real battle for them. When finally the land was purchased a great praise and prayer meeting was held and tears flowed. Then after a year or so the building. There were some interest-free or low-interest loans to pay off which took another five years, but the church had no rent to pay now and as well as the church building there was a manse for the pastor.

We sat in Pastor Nakano's front room with the autumn sun blazing out of a cloudless sky slanting in through the double-glazed window. As usual we prayed first, thanking God for this building in which we could worship Him. We looked at each other, both thinking the same thing: God was a worker of miracles. These bricks, these glazed windows were a testimony to His faithfulness. The pastor drew in his breath through his teeth, grinned and then suddenly quite seriously he said 'Sensei, I have learned what it is to be under-shepherd of the flock through this experience.' I knew what he meant. In all the ups and downs in this battle of faith, for that is what it was, he had at times stood alone. He had encouraged, exhorted, shown patience and exercised faith; he had kept the goal steadily before the church. The event had done something for him also. It had given him an assurance and a depth of character which he hadn't had before. I felt a sudden warming towards him. He was a good man to work with.

Olga and I learned a lot about customs and the way the Japanese think from this pastor. Some of it we had read about, and some we re-learned because we had forgotten it. Yet Japan is a changing nation. So many things have changed. For example, the Japanese have grown taller. When we were first in Japan I could look the whole length of a crowded Underground train compartment — but not now. There are many young men as tall as I — and I am just an inch under six foot. Some people say it's the change of diet — the inhabitants of these islands eat far more meat and cheese and drink more milk than they used to. Others say it is because they have got off the *tatami* — that is to say that they have suites of furniture and arm chairs and sofas, and they sit on these instead. We always tried to go along with the customs and it was in Hirosaki in 1968 that we had our first couch; most Japanese in the modern estate had them by then. It was also the first place in which we moved from a house with un-treated, drab-looking wooden walls to a house of mortar cement, almost a western-style place. It was about that time too that we first had a washing ma-chine, gas oven and TV. In the earliest days Olga had cooked on a charcoal-burning heater, then had a gas ring and she astounded some American Chris-tians one Christmas by roasting a chicken in what amounted to a metal box on the gas ring. The gas came — and still does in many places — in big metal tubes which the Japanese call bombs.

In my early days I was asked by a Japanese friend, that old fireman language teacher of ours in Kutchan, whether I preferred Japanese girls in western dress or kimono. I thought to myself that I was going to get into trouble here if I wasn't care-ful, and hedged a bit. When he insisted, I plumped for kimono, the long colourful flowing robe worn by Japanese women. Seki-san the fireman flushed and got quite angry. He told me that that was because of the bandy legs of Japanese girls which would be revealed by western dress. I changed the subject! At the same time I knew what he meant. In the old days when the Japanese women went out to visit or to work or wanted to get their babies off to sleep or make them burp, they would put them on their backs with the child's legs stretched around the waist of the mother or elder sister. This had the result of making most of them bandy. Of course it was all hidden by the kimono. The men were just as bandy, needless to say.

Very few mothers today carry their children on their backs, and then only for a short period. Many have prams, and the improved state of much of the sidewalks makes this possible — trying to push a pram along the old dirt roads would have been something again! So the present generation is growing up with straight legs and this probably gives them a couple of inches they didn't have before.

Together with the kimono the Japanese used to wear a shaped sock with the big toe divided from the others, and a kind of wooden sandal called a *geta*. Under the sole of the *geta* were two blocks of wood about an inch square, which lifted the wearer off the mud of the street but also tended to give her a short mincing step, the *geisha* of old. Women walking in these *geta* also made a special sound. Although Japanese women rejected the so-called mini-skirt they now wear very stylish western dress — I say western but in fact the designers are Japanese. From only a short distance away it is quite impossible these days to tell a Japanese from a foreigner by his or her dress, height or walk.

The people are very aware of colour. It used all to be decided for them. Little babies wore bright red. Little girls wore pink. Little boys wore blue. When they got to school both boys and girls wore school uniform which was a dark navy blue. The discerning person judged the age of a man or woman by the style and colour of dress. No man, much less a woman, unless she was a street walker, would be seen in red. A general rule was that the older one got the more sedate and drab became one's clothes. It must be all of twelve years ago now that when home on furlough I impressed upon a young lady bound for Japan as a missionary that in no way should she take any red clothes with her. I think that year all the feminine population of Japan from sixteen to sixty decided to wear red. Red skirts, red blouses, red shoes, the lot. Obviously I didn't go up in the estimation of that young lady missionary, who had left a lot of nice red coloured dresses back in England. Now in Japan as far as colour is concerned it seems that anything goes — but does it?

The Japanese never have physical contact with one another in public. Their normal greeting is the bow — the lower the more respectful. If equals are greeting one another then they try to look over the top of their eyebrows to make sure that neither pulls a fast one by getting in an extra bow. Olga and I never showed any kind of affection towards each other in public, not even a handshake, and our speech was quite formal. That's changing now. But the trouble is, I cannot change that quickly. A young male student advanced towards me and his hand went out for the handshake. Too late he realized that the honourable elderly grey-haired missionary was beginning to bow to him in recognition. He hurriedly pulled back the offending hand as though he had put it on a hot stove and went into a hasty dive. By this time I had noticed that hand movement, had checked my bow in mid-air and was putting out my hand in welcome. These actions of hand-pushing and head-dropping were repeated a couple of times until young student and old missionary finally caught up with each other.

Often nowadays one sees young fellows and girls in the shopping arcades or elsewhere going hand in hand, a sure sign that their relationship isn't official. I don't mean that there is anything wrong with it. If they pursue it and have the right educational and family background, then they may approach their parents to get the relationship heading towards marriage. If this should occur they would become much more formal!

How far have the Japanese changed? How western have they become? Do they still ignore an invitation to come in unless it is offered two or three times? Maybe it depends on where you live. Hokkaido is much more free than Tokyo. A young Hokkaido woman moving to Tokyo was snubbed when she accepted an invitation to visit from a Tokyoite. She had been quite sure it was genuine. It may be difficult to convince tourists, but these changes are outward trappings. The inner kernal of culture and values remains the same, all the more so when they see that their relationships are the successful ones in so many spheres — worker and management, for example. Spiritual discipline, loyalty at personal expense, sincerity and obligation are still very much keynotes of society. A oneness of identity is shown in all sorts of situations. One day a beggar — and there are not many now in Japan — came to our door and asked for something, and I gave him a little help. A Japanese Christian visiting us at the time pushed past me very rudely, dashed out into the street and caught the beggar up after a couple of paces. He said, 'How dare you, a Japanese, come begging at the house of a foreigner?' The apology of the beggar was significant to me. 'I am sorry, I didn't realize it was a foreigner. I would not have called.' To him it was a shameful thing to ask something of a foreigner.

It was in our new house in Hirosaki that we learned another lesson. A lady used to come in twice a week in the morning to help out a bit. She was a very pleasant person and cooked delicious *tempura*.[1] One day we discovered we had lost some money. We were quite sure that she had not taken it, in fact I had come into the house with a feeling that there was something wrong, and saw a back window open and the dustbin pulled up under it. It was pretty obvious what had happened. In the course of conversation we mentioned the robbery to the lady, and somehow through this we lost her confidence and friendship, and she made excuses as to why she should not come any more. I suppose that just mentioning it to her implied that we thought she was involved.

It must have been about the time we were saddened by this incident that the phone rang and our Area Director, David Hayman, was speaking to us. 'Come on up to Sapporo, Doug, I want you to act

[1]Fish, meat, vegetables etc sliced thinly and fried in a light batter.

as Superintendent while David Michell is on furlough. You said you wanted to have a go at it.' We
were on the move again.

14
SUPER'S DESK

THE NEW OFFICE building on the outskirts of Sapporo was not much compared with the residences that were to go up around it. In our first winter there the blizzards howled round the building and we had to dig ourselves out regularly to the nearest corner which the snow plough reached. In the next ten years we were to see the city grow in population, style and civic pride. The international Winter Olympics were based on Sapporo four years after we moved up there. This coincided with the opening of the most modern subway or underground railway in the world. The mile-square business centre of the metropolis had its pavements heated underneath so that the snow never lay in the centre of Sapporo. Olga and I had been married in Sapporo in 1954 and our train journey to Tokyo then had taken 26 hours. Just a few years after we moved into the little flat above the office in 1970, a couple of dozen jumbo jets were flying daily between Tokyo and this northern boom town.

When I walked into the small office with its telephone, dictating machine, desk, book-lined shelves and map-covered walls, I had a strong feeling that I was going to be there a lot longer than the year I was supposed to be filling in for David Michell. I was right. For health reasons the Michells never got back to Japan and the missionaries recommended that we continue in the Super's office.

In spite of my assured comment to David Hayman two or three years previously, I wasn't really all that confident about my ability. It seemed as if the job required qualifications in management, a degree in psychology and a knowledge of the culture of half a dozen or more ethnic groups. I had none of these qualifications and felt somewhat insecure in that realm. On the other hand I had been with the work in Japan from the beginning. We had also had younger workers sent to us so that we could show them the ropes, including people from Australia, America, New Zealand and elsewhere. Although we have work among university students, nurses and other special groups like alcoholics, most of our missionary team work in what we call church-planting, and even as a superintendent I could relate to their problems.

The church-planter is attempting to make something out of nothing. Until that 'something out of nothing' materializes the worker is perplexed, praying, pleading with God and crying for blessing. In discussing their first assignment with missionaries in the language school I often heard the comment, 'I do my best work teaching a small group'. Don't we all? But church-planting in Japan means getting out and finding the group that you are going to do your best work with. After the initial excitement of designation to an area or town, house-hunting, farewells, the Superintendent's fond words of encouragement and prayer, the workers are suddenly left in their new home, armed with a degree of proficiency in the language, a few tracts and Gospel portions, a handful of Christian books and the Bible. The missionary faces a population of perhaps fifty thousand very polite but very indifferent people, apparently secure in their own religion and culture. Yet he is aware that he is standing between the living and the dead.

The initial stage is very lonely and it can be humbling also. All the years of training, learning and reading somehow never prepare one for the experience of helplessness that one now undergoes. The young missionary tramps the streets, knocking at doors. He may advertize English Bible classes or cooking and Bible classes, or talk to children and high school kids. After some months there is a small Sunday service. After a year or so maybe half a dozen are coming to the service, but they are never the same half dozen. The missionary wonders if it is lack of language or prayer, cultural barriers or the devil that keeps the people around from believing this glorious Gospel. After three or four years — it may be six or seven — somehow there is a group of twenty or more maturing believers. At that point the missionary hands it all over to a young man out of the Hokkaido Bible Institute, or the Tokyo Theological Seminary, and starts all over again.

When the OMF first went to northern Japan our missionaries were designated to towns of eight to ten thousand people where there was no church,

and which were therefore obviously in need of a witness. But to be honest, we didn't get very far. It
wasn't that the missionaries didn't work hard or
pray, but that by going to those small places we
were taking too much on. For a start, the Japanese
didn't know who we were. They couldn't understand what this foreigner was doing, or what he belonged to. For example, one man approached me
after I had been living in the town for about six
months and said, 'I can't understand what you are
doing. I have been watching you and you do not
seem to be selling anything, and you have brought
no women to the house, and you have had no par-
ties.' He then told me that he was a former member of the Japanese Secret Police! People would ask
us where our Headquarters were and we would say
either Aomori, which to the Japanese is at the end
of nowhere, or Singapore, which was even more of
a puzzle. They could understand the Pope, the
head of the Roman Catholic Church, being in
Rome; but they couldn't understand the OMF in
Singapore.

We didn't seem to relate to a church, and even
people at home have asked me why we didn't work
with the existing church from the beginning. The
question is, which church? At the time we began
work in Japan the church itself was split between
those who had compromised with the militarists
during the war and those who had made a clear-cut
testimony, men like Dr Tsutada who had stood
firm and gone to prison for his faith. It's only now
that we realize how much we were fighting against

the tide at that stage. Nevertheless, thousands of young people heard of Jesus Christ and many high school children were converted; but what happened was that when they left high school they went into the big towns and we lost them. Follow up was difficult due to the reluctance of Japanese, especially young people, to go along to a church they don't know. So gradually the thinking among the missionaries changed and we began to move into the bigger cities such as Hakodate, Asahikawa and Sapporo. It is in Sapporo that we have seen our work thrive the most. In fact it's been thrilling, now that we look back; although it has been hard and slow work, we can now see the results. About the time we decided to move into the bigger cities we also decided to sharpen up our language institution and to start a Bible school.

Not that the work in these small towns was all wasted. Many of the individuals who were reached in those places have become leaders in the growing Japanese Church. Mr Shinada, for example, was then a young man who had a number of problems. To Eva Glass he appeared to be very communistic in his outlook. This was probably because he had read some of the literature current in Japan at that time. He would go along to Eva, who was then a missionary in the fishing town of Mori, and ask her and her fellow workers all kinds of questions. They didn't always understand the questions, but they had him read the Bible, and gradually the work of conviction in his heart increased and he accepted Christ as his Lord and Saviour. The point is, it was definitely the impact of the Bible on him which brought him to this place of repentance. Actually he was a seeker at heart but probably just wanted to show his superiority by asking difficult questions.

Mr Shinada felt that God was calling him into full-time service and he went to the Tokyo Bible Seminary. After he graduated he worked with the Pacific Broadcasting Association in radio and was also the dean of a hostel for university students. When we began our Bible School in Sapporo, with Arthur Reynolds as Principal, we asked Mr Shinada to come to the north again and to work with us. Here again the question of loyalty shows its importance: Mr Shinada had all along felt the desire, or responsibility, to come back to Hokkaido with OMF. So a training programme for workers began, but at first these young men and women who were coming to our Bible School for training were going off to work with other groups; this wasn't a very happy situation for Mr Shinada who had hoped they would help the OMF work forward. He moved from being the Dean and a lecturer at the Bible School to become the Principal, and we began to see the graduates moving into pastoral situations in our groups in the north. Mr Shinada, who was to have such a tremendous influence in the building up of our work in Hokkaido, came to Christ in a small town where fishing was the main industry.

People can prove me wrong, but to me a missionary means an evangelist — an evangelist in a cross-cultural situation. At the same time, the moment someone becomes a Christian then the evangelist is involved in a pastoral and teaching situation. However, the next somewhat illogical step is equating evangelism with street preaching. There were plenty of opportunities for street preaching at first, with or without loud speakers and amplifiers. Most of the younger workers who came to us were initiated into this form of outreach.

I never found street preaching an easy thing to do, but my heart would be moved by the crowds without Christ, so I did it anyway. We used to preach at festivals outside department stores, or wherever people congregated together. Mike and Valerie Griffiths and Olga and I would make a foursome, they giving out tracts and I doing the preaching because I had the most language. Mike hadn't been in Japan very long and although his language was inadequate he had plenty of enthusiasm. While he had tracts to give out to the passing crowds he expected me to keep going. He knew when I was running out of steam because I would start on the last part of my message which was on the two ways, the narrow and the wide.

The four of us were outside the department store in Hakodate one day and I was speaking from a poster on Zacchaeus — wealthy but lonely. A very smart limousine drew up and a man stepped from the back of it and was about to go into the building. Hearing me with my queer accent, he stopped and listened for a minute or two, then — as if aware that men in his walk of life didn't loiter in the street — he hurried in through the swing doors. A week or so later I was out of town, and Mike received an invitation to a cocktail party on board a British Naval vessel which had come into port. Mike had more Japanese language than most of the Naval officers so he had plenty of opportunity to talk to the Japanese who were there. One man looked at him and said, 'Aren't you the man who stood with the foreigner preaching Christ the other day?' It was the man we had seen get from the back of the limousine — he turned out to be the chairman of a shipbuilding company!

Another interesting incident occurred when I was out on the streets of Hachinoe with Allan Knight (who later became our Director for Finance and Administration in Singapore). I was speaking through a microphone, using an amplifier, and Allan was giving out invitations to our church meeting. I noticed him talking to a young woman and afterwards pulled his leg a bit as I asked him about her. It turned out that she was a Christian from another town, who had come to Hachinoe to look after her sister-in-law who was expecting a baby, and her brother who was ill in hospital. Sure enough she came to the church service held in our home, together with her sister-in-law, the following Sunday. The young woman returned to her own home after a month or so but her sister-in-law, together with the new baby, started attending my meetings. Allan and his wife, Shirley, became particularly friendly and close to her, and she became a keen Christian. In the meantime her husband, a taciturn athletic young man, while not showing much interest was not opposed to his wife's new faith. He worked for an electrical company, and they had a small flat in a block of flats owned by the company. She told her friends about Christ, and we decided to have some tent meetings in an area near to the block of flats. The tent was crowded every night with people from the electrical company and we expected to see a great result, so we were quite disappointed when, although they had listened so well, not one of them made any movement toward the Lord. And yet the young husband, who had attended all these meetings and helped us with the equipment, said in a quiet voice to Allan, 'I want to be baptized'. Allan baptized him in a rather stormy sea and we wondered if this was a symbol of the kind of Christian life which the young couple would have.

I was in their flat one evening shortly afterwards when the young man pulled out a letter of about twenty pages of Japanese writing. As I glanced at it I saw that it was in fact a series of questions, beginning something like this: I understand you have become a Christian. What kind of Christian? What do the missionaries believe? Do they believe that the Bible is God's word? And so on for about twenty questions on doctrine and behaviour. I asked the young man who this letter was from and he replied, 'It's from my grandfather.'

I said to him that he hadn't told me his grandfather was a Christian.

He said, 'You didn't ask me.'

He then told me that his grandfather had been one of those early Japanese pioneers going to Europe to learn about western customs and ways. In Germany he had gone along to a Christian Assembly and had there become a believer. All down the years he had prayed for his family. This old man, now in his nineties, lived hundreds of miles from Hachinoe but God had used us to set in motion a series of events which led this young man to Christ.

I don't know that I would advise missionaries to do street preaching today in Japan. Traffic on the streets, the problem of obstruction and the doubt as to whether anyone would stop and listen anyway would rule it out, perhaps. Yet there are people who do. Politicians use large vans well equipped with every kind of amplifier to make their claims.

I dropped in recently at a student meeting in the centre of Sapporo where fifteen or twenty young people were preparing for a meeting that evening. Three of them came around me. 'Mr Abrahams, we understand you're a street preaching expert.' I was duly flattered but disagreed. In any case, I hadn't done any street preaching for some time. 'That's a pity, we were hoping you would give us some examples.' Vaguely I offered to help them some time, but they thought that now was the time.

I looked out of the window. It was ten to six on an autumn evening. The streets outside were crammed with city workers, jostling each other and hurrying for buses or the car parks. I could see that I was not going to escape from my young friends, who were all prepared with a poster, and a board to put the poster on. Within moments we were outside a large bank by the traffic lights. One of the students pointed to the traffic lights and said, 'We have timed the pedestrian lights. Before they change you have one minute to preach the gospel.' Certainly I could see that they had done their homework — I would have a captive audience of nearly a hundred people. I took a deep breath and started speaking with my Bible open. After a time I thought one of the students would take my place, and I looked around for help, but there was none. The university men, with open Bibles, were all talking to individuals. Resigned to my fate I kept the programme going for twenty minutes or so and then stepped down from my perch. 'What were you fellows doing?' I asked them. They explained, rather sheepishly, that when I began to speak people had come up to ask them what that crazy old foreigner was shouting about. They had been very happy to tell them. Perhaps this is what is meant by serving the church in Asia!

House to house visitation is a work I have never found easy. Perhaps one of the reasons is that the men are out at work and we find ourselves speaking to a young Japanese housewife who is often very worried to find this huge foreigner standing there. Today all the sects, such as Jehovah's Witnesses, Mormons and Moonies are active in house to house visitation in Japan. If we do any, we have to make it clear from the beginning that we are the good old Christian church. Hubert Fisher had had many years as a missionary in China before going to Japan. In his late sixties, he would strap a few books and Christian magazines on the back of his bicycle and go from house to house. Hubert explained to me that when the housewife came to the door she wasn't a bit scared of this grey-haired gentleman.

Hubert called at one house and the woman told him gruffly, 'We have a Bible here and my husband's a baptized Christian. He never goes to church and he never talks to me.' And she closed the door. The names of the inhabitants of a house are written up outside on a plaque, so Hubert made a note of the name and passed it on to the resident OMF missionary in the town. This lady made a point of finding the house and visiting it regularly, taking with her as ammunition a Christian magazine, and always making a point of inviting the woman to church. The woman took the magazine but never asked Margriet into her house. However, when Margriet went on furlough the woman felt that now she ought to go to the meeting. She went, and was converted. Filled with joy and peace she went home to her husband and with righteous indignation soundly scolded him for not telling her about the Christian faith she had now come to know. Her husband then started to come to church, and since then a number of the members of the family have been converted. Also he has a senior Christian testimony in the town. But as for me, I dislike house to house visitation.

Cherry blossom evangelism, as we called it, used to be another fruitful way of meeting people. Cherry blossom time in Japan is holiday time. Even in the days when there was little leisure time, and certainly nothing like a week's paid holiday, the farmers and factory workers could reckon on a day off to go out into the country to the nearest cherry viewing place. The area of the cherry blossom trees was always a lively, bustling lighthearted experience, rather like Blackpool or Southend. Stalls selling children's highly coloured plastic toys, booths selling bowls of noodles or strings of meat on sticks, or hot corn on the cob, fruit vendors, fortune tellers and drinks cafes hastily erected. The smaller children would be in bright kimono, girls and boys in uniform, everyone in holiday mood. At night the cherry blossom was lit up by hundreds of coloured electric light bulbs.

In some ways cherry blossom signifies spring after a long winter. However, to the Japanese the cherry blossom speaks of the shortness and apparent fruitlessness of life (this particular tree bears no fruit). The Samurai, that dedicated swordsman, was taught that he might be called upon to die while still young, giving his life for his lord. As a cherry blossom drops from the tree in its colourful glory, so might this young soldier fall in battle at the height of his strength. Nevertheless, the Japanese are nothing if not pragmatic. Get them in the right mood and they will say that the Japanese may go on about the beauties of nature and the significance and meaning of the blossom, but to many of them it doesn't mean that much. When cherry blossom blooms they go out among the trees, buy a crate or two of beer and drink themselves drunk. Usually they are singing, shouting and maybe fighting. The Japanese proverb: *Hana yori dango* means 'Prefer food rather than flowers'.

Hirosaki was a place for the cherry blossom, as

also was Kanagi, and when the crowds were there we would preach to them from morning to night. In Kanagi which was in the country there was an old train that came up the single track and dropped off hundreds of people from the towns. We had a tent, and as they waited for the train to take them home they would come in, cheerful and tired. They had spent all their money and were prepared to sit and listen to a Bible message or learn a song such as 'What a Friend we have in Jesus' In this way we reached hundreds, and occasionally would meet up with some of them later, in the town. People would come to the service in the town, saying that they had heard us speak out in Kanagi during cherry blossom time.

That door is closed now. Just recently I was in the Kanagi area in cherry blossom time, and thought that for old times' sake I would go and have a look. I drove the car over to the area expecting to see the same old sights. Nothing doing. There was the blossom, but no stalls, no crowds, no singing. I suppose the people were all at home looking at the blossom on their colour tellies. I switched off the engine and sat for a bit. Then I saw a couple of Toyota Cedricks drive up. From the two cars I saw perhaps a dozen people pour out. They walked round for a bit, look-up at the cherry blossom. One of them ran back for a camera, then they took pictures, laughing and joking as they posed in groups. I got out of my car, shut the door and walked across. They were a bit surprised to see a foreigner but relaxed when I spoke to them in Japanese. I offered to take a picture of the lot of them, then they wanted one of me in the group. Then they got into their cars and drove away. So this was what cherry-blossom viewing is now — a quick skirmish in the car out from town and then back again. We would need other methods of reaching Japan's crowds.

But in these days the sophisticated and materialistically minded Japanese people are getting used to jumbo jet travel, luxurious hotel foyers, comfortable coffee bars, homes with every modern convenience and the lure of the choice of a dozen TV channels. They are not likely to come out to a draughty tent to be nibbled by mosquitoes while they sit on a hard bench.

Tent meetings as a way of evangelism have probably gone. Hugh Trevor, one of our fellow workers, saw the writing on the wall and tried something different — a Christian Exhibition. He erected a tent in a borrowed open space, and divided the area into three compartments. In the first he had pictures, news reports and books about the present condition of things in the world. In the next he had information, films and so on showing what the Christian church is doing to try to meet the need. For example, where there is sickness there is a Christian hospital, such as the hospital at Manorom in Thailand. In the third section he advertized the Bible, the life of Christ and the way to become a Christian. At first he found there was considerable interest, with hundreds meandering through the tent and Christians having plenty of opportunity to talk about their faith. But interest invariably dropped off.

We used Christian literature from the beginning, and it was a real weapon in our hands — the more so because we had such little language. Most of the books were by western writers translated into Japanese. One of the continuing bestsellers is 'By Searching' by Isobel Kuhn, a simple account of how she became a Christian and battled with some early problems in her faith. Later she went to China as a missionary and worked among the Lisu. Dr Billy Graham's book 'Peace With God' is another popular one.

I have asked scores if not hundreds of Japanese Christians how they first had contact with Christianity, and why they initially went to church. The highest percentage said that the life of a friend, or the invitation of a friend to come to the church, was the way in which they started. Many said that their first contact was by reading a book. Some started by reading the New Testament but were put off by all the foreign names in the first few verses of Matthew's Gospel. However, I heard of one person who read about what he thought was all those men having children, and this quickened his interest so that he kept going.

In answer to my usual question a pastor's young wife told me her story. She had lived for the first sixteen years of her life in a small village in the mountains north west of Tokyo. Her father was a hereditary Shinto priest, whose duties were to officiate at weddings, carry out purification rites when a building was erected, and sell magic charms to the villagers which they put outside their houses or stuck over the portals of their doors at new year. The family lived very simply, having few of this world's goods. But the priest did have a few books, old and musty, which he kept on a shelf. His daughter had never seen him read or even refer to them. But as she entered her early teens she began to read them, for there wasn't much else to do in the long winter evenings. One was a commentary on Romans by Uchiura Kanzo, a well-known Japanese Bible teacher and Christian leader of the early twentieth century. She would kneel down at the low table, under a sixty-watt light bulb hanging by a plain cord from the ceiling, and would try to understand what it was all about. As far as she knew she had never met a Christian, and never seen a church, a Bible or a hymnbook.

At the age of seventeen or thereabouts she went down to Tokyo for nursing training. As the custom was, she and the other young trainees were not allowed out on the street for a couple of months. So she was excited as a kitten as she anticipated her first free day, when she would be able to go out and see something of the great city. The day arrived and off she went down the busy street. She hadn't gone far when she saw across the road a building with a cross on it, and the words in Japanese — 'Jesus Christ Religion, special evangelistic meeting'. In small print it added, 'Everybody is welcome to come in'. She told me her amazement at realizing it was the same Name as in her father's book! Perhaps the people there could answer the strange longings her studies had aroused in her heart. So somewhat nervously she went into the building and was invited to sit down. She sang songs she had never sung before, and heard the Bible read for the first time. Then when the evangelist concluded his message and invited anyone who would like to become a Christian to come forward, forward she went. The evangelist was apparently very puzzled to meet a person obviously well versed — better than he was — in the doctrine of justification by faith! Books have power. Books will always have a part, but the Japanese are now reading less and watching television more.

On Japanese radio and television it is possible to study a dozen foreign languages — French, German, Russian, Chinese, Spanish, as well as English. There are English conversation classes every day of the week on TV or radio, and textbooks for these courses can be bought from any bookstall. Children are speaking English for several hours a week at school, from the time they are eleven years of age. Adult English classes are advertized all over the place. Invariably students have to take examinations in English, in order to get into university. In spite of all this, very few Japanese people can speak English fluently. This is because they study the language as though it were a dead one, with high priority on grammar rather than on speech. So if an English-speaking missionary moves into a district it isn't long before there is a request for English teaching. 'I am going to America for a year — will you help me with conversational English?' 'I have translated this thesis into English — will you check it over for me please?' This is a particularly difficult one as the missionary cannot usually understand the technical terms, even in English! Then, more bluntly, 'What are your fees for teaching English on a personal level?' 'Do you have an English class for beginners?' 'Do you have an English Bible class?' A worker has to make up his mind whether he is going to teach English at all, how he is going to do so and to whom, whether he will charge expenses or not and whether he will teach English Bible.

When we see how some of these serious keen people struggle with our language, we wonder how much of a mess we are making of theirs.

'Do you eat Japanese food?' a bright young lady missionary was asked by a high school boy. 'Yes', came her reply. 'Are you delicious?' 'Yes', said the missionary without batting an eyelid.

A new worker was shocked that we were charging for teaching English, even though he knew that all we earned in this way went into Mission funds. On the other hand national teachers, that is Japanese who teach English privately to supplement their salaries, are very upset if we teach English. Some idealistic brothers and sisters feel that they have come to preach the Gospel, not to teach English. Unfortunately this attitude only puts up a barrier and closes doors to relationships with the nationals. Others, too enthusiastic, have to be warned about the best use of their time. A couple of hours a week of conversational English in a high school gives a missionary a bit of status and sometimes opens doors to the Gospel.

I have had experience of and learned some of the advantages and pitfalls of most of our methods in church planting. My problem now is, how many of these methods are valid today? Can some be adapted? What new methods must we find to make the Gospel meaningful to the Japanese now? Allied to that problem is, how much use is my understanding of the post-war poverty-stricken Japanese culture and customs, in this new materialistically-minded wealthy country? And how different from me are the new workers coming from the homeland today?

15
ALL THINGS NEW?

MR TANAKA DROVE his Honda with practised skill down the broad smooth highway out of Tokyo toward Mikaka City. The bright autumn sun splashed the blocks of high-rise apartments, turning the mattresses drying or airing on the balconies into one large patchwork quilt of colour. As I sat beside Mr Tanaka, relaxed and comfortable, I thought about the ways our paths had crossed. I had met him during that strange missionary interval known as furlough — I had visited his home, been entertained by his Christian wife and studied the Bible with him; later he had been baptized in an English Baptist church. These events formed the unbreakable link between us. I looked across at him. His small frame, gentle appearance and quiet voice did nothing to reveal a very shrewd and tough business acumen and a deep knowledge of modern electronics. I couldn't help thinking how far modern missions had moved from the old concept of pith helmet, Bible and khaki drill suits. This man was in every way my superior, educationally, culturally and in his ability to make his way in the world of today. Yet it was to me he had come with his questions about the purpose of life.

This modern Japan has turned my thinking upside down. On the surface it surely has no need of missions. Medically it is far advanced, culturally it has beliefs which have apparently served it well for fifteen hundred years. In the arts there are painters and playwrights, poets and authors who are internationally known. Educationally, young people leaving high school may well be a year ahead of their European and American counterparts in science and mathematics. Few if any children suffer from malnutrition in this modern country. Economically 80% of the Japanese people are now proud to call themselves middle-class. If traditional missions were to the poor, the ignorant and to those outside medical science, then what have I to offer to this country? Again and again I have had to go back to the Bible for my authority. It is only in the Bible that we see the uniqueness of our Lord Jesus as Saviour and Lord, and the fallen, really needy spiritual state of the human race — and this includes the Japanese.

I glanced again at the untidy suburban landscape as we hummed along in this status symbol of Japan's new technology. Just a few hours before Mr Tanaka's young son had been talking to me. 'I don't even know my father at all. He is out from early morning until late at night. He spends all his time with his Company. What is the use of it all?' The son wanted to study either sociology or psychology at university, but Mr Tanaka was more concerned that his son should study something which would serve him materially in the days to come. There was not too much communication between the two.

For the sake of conversation I reminded Mr Tanaka of some of his recent triumphs in Europe, where he had claimed large contracts. He remarked ruefully that the competition had been very strong, and when I suggested to him that Japan was now well ahead, he shook his head negatively without taking his eyes from the road.

'Europe,' he said, 'is a four-wheeled economy; we Japanese have a two-wheeled economy.' I asked him what he meant.

'Your economy is like a car. Even if it slows down and stops it will not fall over. Our economy, the Japanese, is like a bicycle. We have to keep pedalling because if we stop the bicycle will fall over.'

Whether this is true or not is impossible for me to judge, but it was a revelation to me of the pressure under which these people find themselves. They feel they must keep going.

Back in Sapporo, Olga and I were visiting the home of a veteran missionary couple who were concerned with building up a local church and had contact with a number of young people. The lady was quite distressed. One of the students they knew had parents who were both academically well qualified, one being a professor in the university and the other a high school teacher. They were determined that their son should also do well academically. It was apparent to the missionaries, however, that the course which the young man was taking was too much for him. He moved from one flat to another, trying to find a quiet place, and finally asked the missionaries if he could come and live with them. Although they had encouraged him in other ways they felt that this would be impracticable. A few days later this young man was found dead in the woods at the university, having taken his own life — another sacrifice to the pressure of Japanese society. Of course the missionary was heartbroken and felt that they should at least have tried taking him into their home; but I could not see how they could blame themselves. I sometimes wonder if Japanese people have children to use for their own ends, but then when I think of some happy families I am ashamed of these thoughts.

I advertized in the newspaper, 'A series of lectures on Jesus Christ based on Mark's Gospel, given in a room in the Yomiuri newspaper offices'. The Yomiuri newspaper has a concrete office block in the centre of living, thriving Sapporo. As well as shooting up to the sky, the block goes down two or three storeys below ground level. There, wide passages lead to customer-crammed department stores, eating houses, discotheques and soft-lighted coffee shops. The room we rented for three months was in the area given over to cultural pursuits, where you could learn 'Go' or 'Shogi' (Japanese board games), flower arrangement, tea ceremony or dressmaking. Our particular room, well lit, had space for about twenty chairs, with long narrow tables and a blackboard up front.

Fifteen people registered for the course. Four were already Christians, including a middle-aged lady whose family was opposed to her faith and would not free her to go to worship on Sunday, and a young bride waiting to follow her husband to England. But most of the group had not studied the Bible at all, so to get on their wavelength I attempted to approach it as though I had never read it either. This created a sense of expectancy in the group from the beginning. We quickly discovered that the Kingdom of God had to do with the gift of the Holy Spirit, healing, casting out demons, authoritative teaching and the forgiveness of sin. I had the group memorize certain features. When we were discussing the forgiveness of sin, one upright burly man in his forties, a lieutenant-colonel in the Japanese Self-Defence Force, said in front of them all, 'Surely we all need forgiveness'. When we came to Peter's denial of Christ, one of them said strongly, 'What sort of man was this Peter? No Samurai would deny his lord.' As we read of the trial of the Lord Jesus the group again were incensed — 'Why didn't Pilate release Jesus?' When we came to the resurrection, they went home puzzled yet hopeful.

After one of the sessions the Army officer invited me for a cup of coffee. In the smoke-hazed room with the rock music in the background he turned to me and said he wanted to become a Christian. I pulled my Bible out and we read through some Scriptures together. He has a long way to go, but he has started.

This is a new Japan; the nation is more self assured, more technologically advanced, economically well off. And there are new missionaries coming to Japan these days too, whose thinking and approach to life is different from what ours was when we first came to this country thirty years ago. Although there are single workers, most are coming out married with one or two children. They do not seem to have the same — dare I say it? — arrogance which we had. They have a more gentle approach. By contrast the Japanese themselves are much more open to friendship on an equal level with the foreign missionary. The Japanese today meets the foreigner on equal terms. He has a full social life with tennis clubs, golf clubs, cultural and art classes and swimming clubs. The new missionary can join in all these things, if he can afford it! When we old-timers began there were not many social links which we could forge. Today, on a winter Saturday morning in Sapporo, most of the new workers will be on the ski slopes learning to ski, if they haven't already done so. My old spartan nature reacted a bit to this, but then I realized that they were out on those slopes making real friendships in a natural way. Michael Griffiths, former OMF General Director who himself worked in Japan, once stressed that we should make friendships in our early years in the country. Certainly Olga and I had some Japanese friends, but not as many as we would have liked.

For new missionaries to come out as a family, while perhaps being more natural, does bring its own testings. Both husband and wife need to learn the Japanese language. If the wife avoids this or is not helped in it by her husband, then in two or three years' time she will find herself living on an island, as it were, in the midst of a Japanese-speaking people. If there are one or two small children, then the husband will have to take his turn at all the chores while his wife is doing her language study. Other tests come more quickly too; for example, within two or perhaps three years of arriving in the country the parents face the challenge of the children leaving home to go to school. This is not easy at any time, but when it follows so soon after leaving one's own home country, getting used to life in Japan as well as to OMF and its ways, and perhaps the stress of going out to start new work with inadequate language, this separation puts real pressure on new workers.

I think sometimes they look at us old warriors and think that we are a race apart. Maybe we had some special grace or we had no hearts when we faced up to the children going away to school . . . nothing could be further from the truth. Olga and I, as well as other missionaries, prayed over each child, looked at each one's character and tried to assess what this separation was meaning to the child, and whether he or she could take it. We had to remember at the same time that in going to Nanae, the Chefoo School in northern Japan, the children were going to a place where they were cared for, prayed for, and given a remarkably cosmopolitan education to fit them for life in most of the English-speaking countries. In spite of all this, we felt the separation acutely. I remember driving back from the station after seeing off our two older children, with the third still in the car with me. He turned to me and said 'Why do they have to go away so often?' This triggered this hard-hearted man and the tears ran down his face. A Japanese who was walking along the road caught my eye and to his astonishment saw not only a foreigner — perhaps the first he had ever seen — but a foreigner with a tear-stained face: I shall never forget the embarrassed, if not horrified expression on the man's face as he hurriedly looked away. It cheered me up no end.

The men and women whom God is calling to Japan now are well-trained. They have been taught not to interfere with the culture of the people, nor impose their own background on them, and to shun every form of paternalism. This being so, they are quick to jump on anything which they sense is of that nature. But there are also developments in churches in the West which are not heeded or particularly wanted by the Japanese Christians. One new lady worker was depressed by the apparent formality and slowness of the Japanese Sunday morning worship. She approached a Japanese young man whom she knew spoke some English, and said to him slowly and deliberately, 'Do you not find the Japanese form of worship rather boring?' He looked at her for a moment, summoning up his English words carefully, and replied, 'We Japanese find the worship of God a serious matter'.

Another young worker was very puzzled by older missionaries' delight when a group of Japanese believers put up their own building. 'What's so wonderful about putting up a building? Why not hold house meetings?' This is a growing pattern in the West, of course, but it brings problems in Japan. If fifteen people came to a Japanese home for a meeting, each one of them would bring a present. The hostess would have to note who brought which present, and the general value of the gift, and make sure that next time they met she thanked the giver for the present. She might also feel she must return a gift slightly less in value to each one of the friends who had brought something to the meeting. This kind of formality quickly puts paid to house meetings! Why then has the missionary been successful in starting house meetings and in this way contributed to the building up of the church? The answer is that whether he likes it or not, the Japanese call the missionary's home a *kyokai* — that is, church. They feel free to come to the church, the missionaries' home; and anyway the missionary, being a foreigner, is outside their way of society.

Two or three churches in Sapporo have long, solid-looking pews. A young worker tackled an older worker and demanded to know why these pews had been imposed upon the nationals. With a grin he replied, 'This is their idea of having arrived. If we have pews in our church we have really got something.' The Japanese Christians have their own idea of what a church building should look like. They certainly want to get away from the Buddhist ideas wrapped up in those romantic curving roofs so loved by the tourist. They know how they want to worship and why they want pews!

Yes, the church situation is different today from when we arrived. There is a Bible School, independent churches, experienced helpers. No need now for that awful sinking feeling we used to have when a Japanese enquirer was asking a question in

Japanese we couldn't understand. Help is only a telephone call away. Now we have a group of independent churches with their own conference, choosing leaders and budgeting for evangelistic outreach, Bible School, and overseas missions. Our first-ever Hokkaido conference had consisted of sixty young people with no full-time Japanese workers. Today three hundred turn out for the annual conference, national workers are in the majority, and a young people's camp is held separately. A new missionary just leaving language school may be designated to work with an older worker, a national church leader, or most likely in a pioneer outreach from a local church.

Some years ago I was invited to attend OMF's Overseas Council meetings in Singapore, and Cambodia was on the agenda. An officer of the Cambodian Army on his way back to Cambodia was passing through Singapore, and he spoke to the Council, urging OMF to make Cambodia a priority for Christian workers while there was still time. A keen and sincere Christian, he insisted that the people were open to the Gospel as never before. OMF was able to send a handful of missionaries into the country for the last year before the doors closed.

Back in Sapporo after Council, I spoke to the students at the Hokkaido Bible Institute with Cambodia's need heavy on my heart. I stressed prayer, but a young man sitting at his worn desk heard God call him to the Cambodians that day. The fact that Cambodia soon closed to the Gospel seemed to bring an end to that momentary vision, but while working as an ancillary hospital worker in the south of Japan he was challenged again when he heard of the refugee camps in Thailand. Accepted by OMF's Japan sending committee he is now sweating it out for the Lord among the Cambodians in those camps.

Japan has been sending out missionaries almost from the beginning of its church's history. They went to Korea and Taiwan in the days when those countries were under Japanese dominion, to Brazil and to the western United States to work among their own people. When OMF opened its ranks to Christians of all nationalities, Japanese responded.

I could not help wondering what I was doing in Japan struggling with its language and customs, when first-rate Japanese Christians were going overseas as missionaries! I was invited to a missionary training camp and met thirty or so dedicated young people open to whatever God had for them. There were two of us missionaries among the speakers, and we were the only ones who complained of the highly-suspect fish which was served up to us. It was known as good missionary training! What thrilled me was Dr Hatori's closing message, stressing that if Japanese men and women were to go overseas as missionaries, then they must be none but the best. They should be men and women of deep faith, strong convictions, especially academic qualifications from our best universities. But then, almost as an afterthought, he took a deep breath and raised his voice, no longer needing a microphone, 'But if God has called you like Amos, from the plough or the ricefield to preach His Gospel overseas, then do not disobey His call'. We have gone the full circle. From all nations to all nations.

Mr Hosokawa was worried, and so were his fellow pastors. After 25 years in Hokkaido OMF seemed to be changing its direction. A missionary was being designated to Tokyo. Other missionaries had gone south to work among students, but this was different, this was church planting. Not that there were no needs in the thickly-populated areas in the industrial south from Tokyo to KitaKyushuu, but who would come north if OMF did not? Besides, the OMF was known in the north. The pastors stood round a map of the island, looking at the twenty coloured pins denoting churches. They studied the vacant places. Then at the liaison committee Mr Hosokawa did an unusual thing. He asked if he could speak to the OMF missionary force when they met at their annual conference.

Mr Hosokawa was obviously moved, he had something to get off his chest. He stood before us at the conference with the large map of Hokkaido hanging behind him, and the gist of his argument was that OMF's work in Hokkaido was not finished. Twenty churches was not enough — the goal should be two hundred by the end of the century, if Christ did not return. Mr Hosokawa went on to speak feelingly of all the years of evangelism in the north, of the slow advance at first and now the established goals. New goals must be made. 'Please keep sending new workers to Hokkaido,' he finished, 'and we shall work with them till those goals are reached.'

We were moved. Here was a new call from a national Christian who knew us and who longed to continue to work alongside us. Sometimes I wish I had another thirty years to give to Christ in Japan.

There are about a thousand missionaries in the OMF, including people in home offices in the West . . . but these do not represent the whole of the work which God does through the Fellowship. There are thousands of Christians who know and support this Asian evangelism, and there are many hundreds who pray. These friends meet once or twice a month in groups of maybe a dozen or less, usually in someone's home. Some of us missionaries go in awe of them, for they often know more about what God is doing worldwide through the Fellowship than the OMF members themselves.

I am at an organized rally for these prayer groups in Newcastle. The venue is a church hall and the time is the coffee break between meetings. People are standing around in groups talking, or thumbing through books on the literature stall, or peering at the pictures of work in Asia on display. An old man makes his way across to me, obviously what we call a working man. The first thing I notice about him is his remarkably peaceful face.

'How is Nakagawa?' he asks.

That is like asking how Griffiths is in Wales, or Stewart north of the border. 'Which Nakagawa?' I query.

'Nakagawa the boxer,' he replies.

My mind goes back 25 years to the wooden shack we lived in in Shizunai, where the north Pacific washes the shores of the coast. Nakagawa; the spiritual firstfruits of our married life together in Japan. Nakagawa visiting the house day after day, studying the Bible while I tried desperately to understand his language. Nakagawa demanding to be an evangelist while I insisted that first he should work for his living and show the people of his home town that he had really changed. Nakagawa working with pick and shovel for a year, then starting to preach. Nakagawa getting married to a shy woman who walked with a limp. Nakagawa preaching among the fishermen of the Inland Sea, preaching daily on a radio ministry, visiting prisons, pastor and preacher.

'Pastor Nakagawa is very well and serving the Lord as faithfully and earnestly as ever,' I inform the old man. He literally beams with pleasure. But I am inquisitive. 'Have we ever met before?'

'No, this is the first time.'

'How do you know about Nakagawa?' From the inside pocket of his jacket the man slowly, almost reverently, draws out a folded piece of paper and passes it over to me. I see that it is something the OMF has published years before, with a picture of Nakagawa and me, and short accounts of how we had both come to Christ. The old man is still talking. 'I got that piece of testimony 25 years ago and I have prayed for you and for Nakagawa the boxer ever since. Every Friday morning I have remembered you and him in prayer.'

I was astounded. This dear old brother standing before me in this church hall, never having met me, had faithfully interceded before God for me and for Nakagawa. This was faithfulness; down through all the testings, triumphs and failures of my missionary experience in Japan this brother had held on to God for me like Moses held on for Joshua when Joshua faced the Amalekites.

After seven years in Japan I suddenly developed severe attacks of asthma which would begin in the evening and go on till morning. Olga was desperate. I would be rushed to the hospital in the middle of the night. I was sleepless and exhausted. During those days this friend was praying. On furlough it was decided that we should not return because of my malady. A woman loaned us her house by the sea and when I went for another medical the doctor decided I could return to Japan after all. When we felt the wrench of leaving our children in England this brother was praying down God's comfort. When we needed money to have our children visit us during their holidays the Lord supplied, but this brother was on his knees for us.

When I despaired of results and felt that I couldn't go on and sent in my resignation, this old man was in the secret place with the Father. When there were strange fierce temptations which, if succumbed to, would mean the end of a testimony, unknowingly strength was coming through this man's prayers.

During the years when the radio programmes began, the Hokkaido Bible Institute began, churches were growing and buying land and buildings and calling pastors, and we were part of the team that experienced it all — this brother who had never seen the rice fields and misty mountains of Hokkaido had been involved in it.

Feeling a great lump in my throat and tears beginning to rise, I said 'Thanks very much,' and shook his hand.